# Weddings from the Heart

# Weddings from the Heart

## Ceremonies for an Unforgettable Wedding

Daphne Rose Kingma

**Conari Press**
**Berkeley, CA**

Special thanks to Julie Bennett whose wonderful
idea this was, and to M.J.R. who was,
as usual, incredible

WEDDINGS FROM THE HEART: CEREMONIES FOR AN UNFOR-
GETTABLE WEDDING Copyright © 1991 by Daphne Rose Kingma

Printed in the United States of America on recycled paper

ISBN: 0-943233-21-6

Cover by Andrea Sohn Design; illustration by Tina Cash.

Library of Congress Cataloging-in-Publication Data

Kingma, Daphne Rose
        Weddings from the heart : ceremonies for an unforgettable
wedding
        /Daphne Rose Kingma. —1st ed.
                p.   cm.
        ISBN 0-943233-21-6 : $9.95
        1. Marriage service—United States.   I. Title.
HQ745.K48  1991
392'.5—dc20                              91-26762
                                CIP

First edition
1 2 3 4 5 6 7 8 9 10

For
Yvan and Dominique
whose unforgettable wedding was the inspiration

# *Contents*

# Your
# Unforgettable Wedding

*T*his little book is a compendium of weddings from the heart, designed for those of you who desire above all to have a wedding that touches your heart and changes your life, a wedding that you will feel the profoundest sense of joy in recalling, long after the confetti or rose petals have been swept from the driveway.

A wedding from the heart is a ceremony that springs from deep feeling and arouses deep feeling in all those who participate in and witness it. A wedding from the heart is a sacred chalice for your love, an elegant frame for the portrait of two lovers united by high hope, profound emotion, and a willingness to honor their relationship by expressing it as a freely made commitment in the company of family and friends.

More than a mere formality, and not

necessarily traditional, a wedding from the heart is a truly emotional experience, one borne up on a flood of feeling rather than homogenized through the heavy-handed application of tradition. This kind of wedding has as its hallmark the belief that your relationship is a treasure and that your wedding day will be one of the most precious days of your life. In creating a wedding from the heart, you recognize that your wedding is a symbol of your love and that it can be a deeply moving experience for everyone involved, even those who plan and organize it.

A wedding from the heart is more about what you say, do, and feel, than what you wear or how many courses you serve at the reception dinner. It's about love and not about impressing people; it's about your love—what it means to you, where you want it to take you, and what hopes you have for it.

This is not to say that your beautiful dress and the exquisite flowers aren't important, nor that you shouldn't have a traditional photograph of you feeding your new spouse a piece of wedding cake. What it does mean is that you will do these things only because they have meaning for you two, because they genuinely reflect what you feel, because they speak to your heart.

A ceremony is a special event that contains formal or ritualized components, and which has as its purpose the setting apart and elevating of a particular person or event. We have ceremonies to acknowledge achievements, victories, heroes, sorrows, and losses, but of all the ceremonies the wedding is the sweetest because it is a celebration of love. It celebrates possibilities and its mood is hope.

However, for all too many of us the special and beautiful possibilities of the marriage ceremony become gradually eclipsed by the demands of organizing the wedding itself. The endless phone calls, decisions, and expenses involved in planning the event often leave us feeling like the frazzled producers of an off-Broadway musical about love and romance instead of participants in a sacred ceremony that celebrates the power of love and the meaning of this particular relationship.

Weddings can get so bogged down in the endless exigencies of organizing and planning that the experience itself, when it finally occurs, can seem as if it has very little to do with the love that inspired it. You can get so involved with the rehearsal dinner, the bows on the aisles, and the band at the reception that you forget that the most important part of the wedding is the ceremony itself—the words that are said, the promises you make to one another as you bond your life with your beloved in the marriage ceremony.

Of course you want your wedding to flow smoothly; it will. So don't lose the spirit of the day by getting overwhelmed by endless details and allowing yourself to get disconnected from what your wedding is really about—the love you have for the person you are going to marry and the life you want to share.

Everyone wants their wedding to be beautiful, but more than that you want your wedding to be unforgettable, an occasion that, when called to mind, or relived in photographs or on video, will bring you once again into the presence of the moving, exuberant, tender, passionate, and life-changing feelings that caused you to fall in love in the first place. For long after the champagne bottles have been taken away and you've polished off the last piece of frozen wedding cake, it is the essence of your ceremony—the words that were spoken, the atmosphere you created through them, and the love and joy you generated through all the special moments of your ceremony—that will have taken root in your hearts and formed the foundation of a love so strong that it can truly span your life.

Therefore if you want your wedding to be unforgettable you will want to fashion it in such a way that it reflects the uniqueness of your relationship, your hopes, and your experience. Just as you love the person you are about to marry because he or she is in some way different from all others in your eyes, so you want to make your wedding unforgettable by creating a ceremony that is as special as the two of you, one which is tailored to express the feelings, wishes, and intentions that are as singular as you are.

Thus, while the classic image of a traditional wedding—the bride in white and the groom in a tuxedo saying vows of "till death do us part"—is indelibly imprinted on all our minds, it may neither fit your particular circumstance nor embrace the range of feelings you want to evoke as the memento of your love. A wedding, in whatever form, symbolizes and celebrates an emotional and spiritual bond; and you want yours to reflect the love that has affected you so deeply that you have decided to change the whole color and texture of your life by getting married.

This book is a gift to that purpose. First, by providing you with a selection of ideas and elements, it invites you to consciously create the wedding ceremony that will have profound meaning for you. Second, it offers five ceremonies that give you an opportunity to develop one that reflects the uniqueness of your love more precisely than the traditional wedding ceremony can. In this way you can create a ceremony that is truly unique to you and to your relationship and which, therefore, will give you the greatest sense of joy when you recall it. For in saying words that come from your heart and in speaking to the heart of your beloved, you will touch the hearts of all those who share this day with you, making your wedding truly unforgettable.

These ceremonies can be used by any couple who choose to honor their union by getting married, no matter what their sexual or lifestyle preference. Our focus here is on the power of love to bind us together; to transcend the differences that all too often divide us. It is the power of relationship itself we are celebrating, not the specific configuration of it.

Although each ceremony offered here stands complete in itself, as you study them you may find that you would like to use a particular one in its entirety or combine selections from several. They are here for the using, as you desire, to create from them the unique set of words that will makes yours a truly unforgettable wedding.

# Reflections on Marriage

Marriage is the joining of two lives, the mystical physical and emotional union of two human beings who have separate families and histories, separate destinies and tragedies. It is the merging and intermeshing not only of two bodies and two personalities, but also of two life stories. Two individuals, each of whom has a unique and life-shaping past, willingly choose to set aside the solitary exploration of themselves to discover who they are in the presence of one another.

In marriage we marry a mystery, an other, a counterpart. In a sense the person we marry is a stranger about whom we have a magnificent hunch. The person we choose to marry is someone we love, but his depths, her intimate intricacies, we will come to know only in the long unraveling of time. We know enough about our beloved to know that we love him, to imagine that, as time goes on, we will come to enjoy her even more, become even more of ourselves in her presence. To our knowledge we add our willingness to embark on the journey of getting to know him, of coming to see her, ever so wonderfully more.

Swept up by attraction, attention, fantasy, hope, and a certain happy measure of recognition, we agree to come together for the mysterious future, to see where the journey will take us. This companionship on life's journey is the hallmark of marriage, its natural province, its sweetest and most primal gift. To be married means we belong with someone else, that we are no longer always alone, that we no longer must eat and sleep, dream, wake, walk, talk, think, and live alone. Instead there is a parallel presence and spirit in all that we undertake. We are bridled, connected, attended. We move in the midst of the aura, the welcoming soul-filling presence of another human being, no longer facing the troubling, heart-rending hurts of our lives in isolation. In marriage we are delivered from our most ancient aloneness, embraced in the nest of human company, so that the sharp teeth of the truth that we are born and die alone are blunted by the miracle of loving companionship.

Marriage is also the incubator of love, the protected environment in which a love that is personal and touching and real can grow, and, as a consequence of that growth, develop in us our highest capabilities as loving human beings. We are each still and always becoming, and when we marry, we promise not only our own becoming but also our willingness to witness and withstand the ongoing becoming of another human being. That is because in marrying, we promise to love not only as we feel right now, but also as we intend. In marriage we say not only, "I love you today," but also, "I promise to love you tomorrow, the next day, and always."

In promising always, we promise each other time. We promise to exercise our love, to stretch it large enough to embrace the unforseen realities of the future. We promise to learn to love beyond the level of our instincts and inclinations, to love in foul weather as well as good, in hard times as well as when we are exhilarated by the pleasures of romance.

We change because of these promises. We shape ourselves according to them; we live in their midst and live differently because of them. We feel protected because of them. We try some things and resist trying others because, having promised, we feel secure. Marriage, the bond, makes us free—to see, to be, to love. Our souls are protected; our hearts have come home.

In simple terms, this means that because we are safe in marriage we can risk; because we have been promised a future, we can take extraordinary chances. Because we know we are loved, we can step beyond our fears; because we have been chosen, we can transcend our insecurities. We can make mistakes knowing we will not be cast out, take missteps knowing someone will be there to catch us. And since mistakes and missteps are the stuff of change, of expansion, in marriage we can expand to our fullest capacity; in marriage we can heal.

Since life is movement, the passage of time equals change. Therefore, when we promise time to one another, we are putting ourselves in the midst of an infinity of change. Implicitly this is also a promise to expand. We will not be cardboard men and women. We will be electric human beings with variegated histories and fabulous unknown futures.

For marriage is more than just the sentimental formalizing of a feeling; it is a vote of confidence, indeed of conviction, that the romantic feeling of love will be enlarged to encompass far more than itself, that both persons will be able, in time, and within the sacred circle of marriage, to infinitely expand.

Change compounded is transformation, and one of the ultimate consequences of marriage, therefore, is transformation. For so long as we live out our lives in the context of another human being, the changes that accrue in us, that are indeed inspired, required, cajoled, and beaten out of us by our interactions with another—all these will result, in time, in a major transformation of our selves. We literally would become someone quite different without the person we have married, for it is the alchemy of the relationship itself that transforms us. That which we become in the presence of another person—the person we love most deeply, the person we choose to marry and spend our whole life with, the person in whose presence and as a result of whose actions and inactions, words and silences causes us to change, ultimately to transform—brings us inescapably into the being of our highest selves. We become who we were meant to be.

It is precisely at the point at which marriage, the institution, and love, the emotion, intersect that there exist some of our greatest emotional and spiritual possibilities. For marriage is love in the round; marriage is loving in every direction. We marry not only in order to be loved, to be consoled through the miracle of company, to feel secure, to have a place and a person to whom we can come home, to have our own needs met; we marry also to come into the presence of our own capacity to love: to nurture, to heal, to give, and to forgive.

Marriage is the fearless fathoming of our own depths, a coming face-to-face, in the dark mercurial waters of our endless self-involvement, with the jewel-like treasures of our own sub- merged capacities for compassion. For love received is needs met; but love delivered is compassion, is the human spirit altered, is our own most whole becoming. In loving, we are encouraged out to the limits of our most exqui- site human possibilities.

Thus marriage is an invitation to tran- scend the human condition. For in stepping beyond the self-focus of wanting only to have our own needs met, in schooling ourselves in the experience of putting another human being and his or her needs in a position of equal value to our own, we touch the web of transcendence, the presence of the divine.

For loving one another is the beginning of compassion, and compassion generalized is participation in the divine, that experience of life and of the world that paradoxically submerges us in all that exists while at the same time elevating us above it. The compassionate, soul-changing loving of a single other human being connects us most profoundly to the All. And it is in the practice of this radiant other-discovering love that true marriage calls forth the best in us, the most we can ever become.

# Creating Your Ceremony

*T*here are only two elements essential to a legally binding wedding: the vows or promises you make to one another and the proclamation by the officiant that you are now married. All other elements are optional. Therefore in planning your wedding and deciding what you may want to include, you have tremendous freedom to create a ceremony that is totally expressive of you two.

A wedding is the social portal to married life, a turning point, a marker on the path of your own development that denotes the moment at which you cease to be a solitary person pursuing an individual life and begin to take up the joys and responsibilities of sharing your life with another person. Therefore, as you plan the wedding that will stand forever in your memory as the emblem of the moment that delivered you to your new life, you may want to contemplate the meanings of marriage itself. In this way you can discover exactly what you would like to include in your ceremony so it will carry the unique and beautiful meanings that you want to express and hold in memory.

To help you design the perfect wedding, you will also want to keep the following things in mind:

1. What do you want to say about your relationship in this public forum? What stories about it do you want to tell? What beliefs about a relationship do you want to reveal?

2. Since your wedding ceremony is the public blueprint for what you expect and hope for your marriage, what do you want to say about the meaning of marriage both for your own benefit and for that of the gathered guests? (Here you may want to keep in mind that a wedding is also a teaching ceremony for those who witness it.)

3. What is the style of your ceremony and what is the image you want to create through it? A theatrical performance, a intimate conversation,

a religious ritual, a carnival or festival, a gathering of clans, a formal social event?

As you begin the decision-making process, you will want to enlist the counsel of the person who is officiating at your ceremony, first to see if he or she is comfortable with the kind of ceremony you are envisoning, and also to find out if he or she has any suggestions for you. In choosing this person you want to be sure that he or she is willing and able to accurately reflect what you want your ceremony to convey.

There are a number of traditional wedding ceremonies, each with its own specific components. From these I have chosen the twelve elements that I believe have particular meaning for couples today. They are: the Convocation, the Invocation, the Readings, the Address, the Consecration, the Expression of Intent, the Vows, the Blessing and Exchanging of the Rings, the Pronouncement of Marriage, the Kiss, and the Benediction.

You'll notice that I have not included, among other things, the giving away of the bride or the famous "If anyone present has objections to this union, speak now or forever hold your peace." These spring from outdated notions, one viewing a woman as her father's and/or husband's possession, the other granting to the community the right of conferring ultimate approval of a marriage. Neither of these are in keeping with the belief that marriage is a bond of freedom, a truly democratic enterprise, and therefore I have eliminated them. Of course if you choose to include these traditional moments in your ceremony, you can fold them in among the elements which have been included here.

I have also specifically not included music as one of the elements of the ceremony. I am assuming you will want to use music—both at the beginning and end, and liberally throughout the ceremony. You will find that the spoken portions of the ceremony will resonate their meanings to a higher and lovelier degree when they are set off by music. Music creates a meditative and reflective mood, and when placed in juxtaposition to the spoken word, enables you and your audience to feel even more deeply the meanings of what has been said. Music is particularly effective as a kind of meditative punctuation after the Readings, the Address, and the exchanging of the Vows.

Choose the music with the intent of having each selection be an expression of some unique aspect of your relationship, a reflection of something you've experienced together or of the hope you hold for your marriage. Music, whether vocal or instrumental, live or recorded, speaks directly to our souls and adds a richer dimension to the ceremony.

Also, many weddings include a celebration of the Mass or Holy Communion, but since these are very traditional in both content and form, I suggest you use the order of service from your church if you choose to incorporate the eucharist sacrament in your marriage ceremony. Your minister or priest can tell you where they belong.

The entire wedding ceremony is a process of spiritual movement. In its format it leads us from the general to the specific. The ceremony begins with a gathering together of the community and then, through a progression of words and music, directs our focus ever more intently upon the couple until, in the reciting of the vows, we witness their most intimate conversation.

Bearing this in mind, you will want to choose the components of your ceremony with great care. The truly moving wedding ceremony will intentionally follow a form that takes those of us witnessing it from outside ourselves—what we were doing this morning, what we have to do tomorrow—and draws us very intimately into the presence of the love that you two share. Understanding what purpose each element of the ceremony serves can help you choose which parts you want to include and which you would prefer to omit, and therefore a brief description of each of the ceremonial elements follows.

# The Ceremonial Elements

## The Convocation

*T*his is the ceremonial gathering together of you two as a couple with the family and friends you have chosen to share this occasion, to join you in celebrating, acknowledging, and honoring this day and the vows you are making. Here the whole company is called upon to create a ceremonial bond of love around you, a halo of love that will encircle you through all the years of your marriage.

The intent behind this portion of the ceremony is to demonstrate that you are not only affirming your love to the person you are choosing to marry, but also that you believe in it so strongly you want to express your gratitude, hopes, expectations, and commitment in the presence of witnesses. What is being acknowledged here is that the people attending your wedding are not just observers chewing popcorn in the grandstands; by their presence they are bearing high witness to and setting a seal of approval on your marriage. Their attendance confirms the reality of your intentions. That they shared this most important of all days with you is a memory that will support you through the coming days of your life; it is the Convocation that calls them to this privilege.

## *The Invocation*

*T*hese are the words through which you call on God, or whatever outside, higher, or more radiant presence you choose to acknowledge, to witness the ceremony. The purpose of the Invocation is to put you into a meditative and reflective frame of mind, to focus your attention on the fact that what you are undertaking is serious, life-changing, and powerful. It asks you to contemplate whom or what you call upon as your highest witness as you walk upon the path of marriage. For many, this higher presence is

God; for others, it is a higher self who is asked to witness the lofty purpose to which you now willingly submit your selves and your relationship.

Whatever power you invoke here, the Invocation invites you to put yourself in the presence of the holy, to acknowledge that as a couple you stand in relationship to all that is. It acknowledges that you are sanctifying your relationship not only to one another but also in the presence of the divine; it invites you to take your place, through marriage, in the human stream.

## The Readings

*I*n this part of the ceremony the officiant reads one or more selections you have chosen. The Readings are designed to inspire contemplation, to invite you and your witnesses to expand your views about love and marriage. I have included some selections from the Bible, from the classics, and various other sources, but you may want to make selections of your own.

The purpose of the Readings is to introduce into your ceremony reflections on the meaning of love and marriage that have spoken to people over the ages or that say something of particular significance to you. If you make a selection from the classics, you will be choosing words that have been used at a multitude of nuptial celebrations and which carry the rich patina of having moved the hearts of many lovers. Thus in using them, in hearing them spoken at your wedding, you will bind yourselves to the great tradition of marriage and to the celebrations of husbands and wives from other times and places.

If you'd rather be more personal, however, be willing to be adventurous: choose your favorite poem, the words on a card you once sent him, or a love letter she tucked under your pillow. The point is that the selection should reveal something particular about you two. By having such a personal selection read aloud, you open a door for your witnesses, inviting them into the intimate magic of your union. In any case, the Readings provide an opportunity to reflect on the many meanings of love and commitment and generally introduce the theme that will be revealed in the next portion of the wedding.

## *The Address*

*T*he Address, frequently called the homily or sermon, constitutes a message of celebration and exhortation by the officiant at your ceremony, the person you have chosen to teach and inspire you, to set the cornerstone of meaning for the new life you are stepping into. The purpose of the Address is twofold: to deliver a message that is directed to you personally, and to inspire in your guests the meaning of love and the value of marriage.

This is an opportunity for you to add some dimension to your wedding, to have someone express what you really believe and feel about the meaning of marriage. Therefore, in planning the Address with your officiant, you will want to bring to his or her attention not only what is important to you about your relationship thus far but also what you hope to accomplish by getting married.

It is traditional for the officiant to give his or her own sermon, but I am including these Addresses because they enable you to contemplate the landscape of marriage through a variety of lenses, and to direct the officiant toward the view that you want expressed. The Addresses offered here are brief and focus on particular aspects of marriage. You may ask your officiant to use them as a springboard, or you may wish to have one of them read as is to serve as the whole or a part of the Address at your ceremony.

If you prefer to give your officiant free rein with the Address, you may wish to use a selection from any Address or from Reflections on Marriage as one of the Readings in your ceremony.

## *The Consecration*

*T*he words of the Consecration follow the Address and serve to underline and elevate the message you have just heard. To consecrate means to make holy, and in this section of the ceremony, the officiant once again draws attention to your exalted undertaking. Having heard the words of inspiration and instruction, you now prepare to make the promises that will express your desire to fulfill the meaning of marriage as it has been expressed in the Address.

Whether of exhortation or of prayer, the words of the Consecration remind you that what you are undertaking is sacred, and charge you to give serious attention to the commitment you are about to make. They also serve as a transition from the teaching and exhorting part of the ceremony to the more intimate part in which you make your promises to one another. They lead us from those parts of the ceremony that are equally shared by the witnesses and the celebrants, to focus our attention directly on the individuals who are getting married.

## *The Expression of Intent*

*H*ere you are invited to make public your desire to wed. Having heard about the challenges, demands, and joys of marriage in the previous portions of the ceremony, you now state publicly that you intend to go forward with the making of your promises. Like the Consecration, the Expression of Intent calls your attention to the seriousness of the promises you are about to make, the state you are about to enter into. But here, rather than being instructed, encouraged, or forewarned, you acknowledge aloud your intention to go forward.

## *The Vows*

*T*he Vows, of course, are the part we remember most about any wedding ceremony. Your vows are the emotionally and spiritually binding part of the ceremony. Vows are love made tangible. They both reach from and speak to the heart. They advertise the love that brought you together, and draw a blueprint for the love you intend to nurture.

Your vows are more than a bouquet of pretty words spoken in the presence of your witnesses. They are your heartfelt spoken promises of what you are willing to do for one another, under what circumstances, and for what length of time. As you speak these words, you are making yourself accountable through intention—to yourself and to your beloved—to live, love, and behave in certain specified ways. Regardless of whether in time you are able to live your vows to perfection, what you say here is of the utmost importance; for spoken and witnessed, these words will continuously call you to the emotional, behavioral, and spiritual commitment that from this day forward you are choosing to undertake.

The Vows offered here represent both an expansion and a revision of the traditional Vows in that they include some very specific promises about the nature of the union you are entering into. They are tailored to the particular kinds of ceremonies presented here; once again you may want to use them exactly as they are written here or as a basis for formulating your own vows.

In either case, I suggest that during the ceremony you consider reading them in their entirety instead of repeating them after the officiant. You may want to write them out in advance and carry them with you or have one of your attendants hand them to you at the appropriate time. Reading them yourselves will more deeply connect you to their meaning, and, because you are making these promises in the presence of witnesses, they will take on even greater significance.

I also suggest that when you say your vows you turn directly toward one another and recite them face-to-face, instead of facing the officiant. You'll be amazed by the effect that expressing your promises directly to each other can have on the bonds you are making as well as by the intense feeling this soul-to-soul encounter will arouse in you both.

Because the Vows are such a precious and important part of the wedding, at the back of this book I have also included several additional vows that you may be inspired by and prefer to use.

## *The Blessing and Exchanging of the Rings*

*W*edding rings are the material symbol of the bond that is created in marriage, and since you will wear your rings from your wedding day onward, the words that are spoken about them and consequently the meaning that is embodied in them through the wedding ceremony are of the greatest importance. More than anything else in the ceremony, the rings are what you will take with you. The flowers will wilt, and the reception will end, but your wedding ring will be there to remind you day after day that you are loved, that you have been chosen.

Therefore you will want to make sure that the Blessing spoken by the officiant and the words you choose to speak at the time you exchange your rings express most purely the meaning you want to live with every day you wear them.

## The Pronouncement of Marriage

*T*he Pronouncement of Marriage is the public proclamation that you are married, and the presentation by the officiant of you as husband and wife. This is a lovely and special moment, the archway of words through which you now enter the community. No longer solitary, from now on formally bonded to one another, you have passed through the portal to married life.

## The Kiss

*N*eed I say more? This is the delicious part of the ceremony, the moment in which you claim one another with a kiss.

The Kiss seals the promise. The Kiss signifies reverence. Traditionally a kiss confers not only greeting and honor but also attachment. One salutes and claims whomever he or she kisses, so the Kiss is more than a delightful public display of the physical affections that complement the marriage; it is the way in which the groom claims the bride as his forevermore, the way in which the bride claims the groom as forever hers.

## *The Benediction*

*T*he Benediction is the final ceremonial flourish of the wedding. With these words, you, the newly married couple, are sent off with a blessing to halo your union through the long days of the future. The Benediction is buoyant; it offers you good wishes, mirth, joy, exuberance, and maybe one final fillip of exhortation as you set sail for the world.

This is a brief but delightful and rousing moment, the climax of all the excitement, seriousness, and loveliness that has been unfolding in the marriage ceremony. It should be joyous, boisterous, exuberant, and should be followed immediately by jubilant recessional music.

# A Selection of Ceremonies

*A* wedding is one of those rare opportunities we have to experience ritual in our lives, an encounter with the extraordinary in the midst of ordinary life that truly elevates our spirits and brings us into the presence of the holy. Weddings remind us that our lives have meaning and that love is the strongest bond, the happiest joy, and the lovliest healing we can ever experience. It is these notions that form the heart of the ceremonies here, but each ceremony also carries an individual emphasis, a special point of view.

That's because there are a great many aspects to the commitment of marriage. Exactly what you want your wedding to express will depend on your circumstances and your history, your values and your intentions, your view of life, and your beliefs about relationships. Your wedding is the single most special opportunity you will ever have to say to each other in the company of people who love you just how much your relationship means to you, and what path you are laying out for your future.

Therefore, as you go about planning your wedding, I suggest that you read through all the ceremonies before making your selection. See which one seems to capture not only the mood but also the point of view which best communicates what you want your ceremony to express; then use it or adapt it so that it becomes truly expressive of your own feelings and philosophy.

The first wedding, which I am calling *The Marriage of Love and Commitment,* is a revision of the traditional Christian ceremony that acknowledges God as the author of love and the architect of the spiritual commitment of marriage. Here, revised, it offers the blueprint for a sacred union expressed in a more contemporary form, keeping to the spiritual values but expressing them in more modern language.

The second ceremony, *The Marriage of Love and Purpose,* focuses on the deep psycho-

logical meanings of marriage. It acknowledges
that in choosing our partners and in coming
together in marriage we make no mistake, that
we build relationships to heal our emotional
wounds and to lead us toward the fulfillment of
the highest purposes in our lives.

The third ceremony, *The Marriage of
Love and Rejoicing,* is for the ecstatic and light-
hearted among us who want to express in an
exuberant, spontaneous, and perhaps less con-
ventional manner their inestimable joy at finding
their own true love. The spirit of this ceremony is
lighter, sweeter; this ceremony easily adapts to an
outdoor mountaintop wedding, a wedding on
the Staten Island Ferry, in your artist friend's loft,
or your own backyard.

The fourth ceremony, *The Marriage of
Love and Fulfillment,* is designed especially for
those who have been married before. When we
marry a second (or third, or even fourth) time,
we recognize that we have been brought to this
place of fulfillment by everything that has gone
on before. And either specifically or in a general
way, we honor both where we've come from and

where we are headed.

In addition, we instinctively want to create a ceremony that separates us from a mere repeat of the marriage—or marriages—we had before, the marriage(s) that didn't last till the end of our lives. We want to dignify, clarify and celebrate the uniqueness of the present union, and the hopes we hold for it. We want to create a ceremony that will allow us to believe afresh that this marriage is a true bond, that this ceremony honors a profound relationship that has a foothold in the future.

Finally, I have included a ceremony for those who are in recovery from an addiction. *The Marriage of Love and Renewal* is a special celebration for those to whom marriage is one of the highest rewards of a serious commitment to the process of self-healing. This ceremony acknowledges the suffering and uniqueness of that difficult past and celebrates with joy the love that is the legitimate birthright of its future.

Once again, you can use any ceremony verbatim or mix and match the elements from several ceremonies. But however you arrange it, my sincerest wish for you is that you will have the wedding of your dreams, a wedding from your heart.

# The Marriage
# of Love and Commitment

*A*mong its many dimensions, marriage is a spiritual enterprise. For the highest spiritual purpose of marriage is the embodiment of love; and love, as we know, is the strongest power there is. Love is the power that can truly change the world. Since we are so well acquainted with the emotional and social aspects of marriage, we often overlook its loftier dimensions. Yet it is because at some level we do sense that love is its true essence that we make our weddings such special events, and that in our unconscious myths we hold marriage to be the most significant bond that we can ever make.

Recognizing this at least intuitively, we know that we are called to marriage by no mistake, to participate in it as a gift in service not only to the fulfillment of the highest purposes in ourselves but also to the creation of a loving union. We sense that the real meanings of marriage lie far beyond the specific tasks that we will undertake in it, even beyond what we create in one another through it. Through marriage we invite the development of our highest spiritual selves, that which is transcendent in us, that which participates in the pure experience of love.

In this spiritual view, marriage is the human union which replicates and symbolizes the relationship of God to human creatures, of love ethereal and eternal to life temporal and material. In holding these meanings for us, marriage invites us to examine our deepest beliefs, not only about relationships, but also about the power of love itself. It encourages us to allow our relationships to embody the highest values we can hold.

## *The Convocation*

We are gathered here in the presence of God and of this company to join in holy marriage ____ and ____ and to bear witness to the transforming power of love.

Love is a quality of spirit and an attitude of the emotions, but a marriage is a life's work, a spiritual art form. Therefore this is an occasion of both profound joy and great responsibility, and we who partake in it bind ourselves as witnesses to the labor of love that ____ and ____ are undertaking here.

In acknowledgement of this holy purpose and of the power of this occasion, let us pray.

## *The Invocation*

God of Light, who gives us the longing for love and the capability of loving, we give you thanks for ____ and ____ for their open hearts and willing spirits, and for the example of love that they embody here in our presence.

Be with them on this joyous occasion of

showing their love and making their vows; and be with us, their witnesses, that we may all be changed by what is said and witnessed here.

## The Readings

### Colossians 3, 12-14

Put on then, as God's chosen ones, holy and beloved, compassion, kindness, lowliness, meekness, and patience, forebearing one another, and, if one has a complaint against another, forgiving each other; as the Lord has forgiven you, so you must also forgive. And above all, put on love, which binds everything together in perfect harmony.

### Sonnet 116

Let me not to the marriage of true minds
Admit impediments; love is not love
Which alters when it alteration finds,
Or bends with the remover to remove.
Oh no! It is an ever-fixed mark

That looks on tempests and is never shaken;
It is the star to every wand'ring bark,
Whose worth's unknown, although
      his height be taken.
Love's not Time's fool, though rosy
      lips and cheeks
Within his bending sickle's compass come;
Love alters not with its brief hours and weeks,
But bears it out even to the edge of doom.
      If this be error and upon me proved,
      I never writ, nor no man ever loved.
      *William Shakespeare*

### *First Corinthians 13*

Though I speak with the tongues of men
and of angels, and have not charity, I am become
as sounding brass, or a tinkling cymbal.

And though I have the gift of prophecy,
and all knowledge; and though I have all faith so
that I could remove mountains, and have not
charity, I am nothing.

And though I bestow all my goods to
feed the poor, and though I give my body to be

burned, and have not charity, it profiteth me nothing.

Charity sufferth long, and is kind; charity envieth not; charity vaunteth not itself, is not puffed up,

Doth not behave itself unseemly; seeketh not her own, is not easily provoked, thinketh no evil;

Rejoiceth not in iniquity, but rejoiceth in the truth;

Beareth all things, believeth all things, hopeth all things, endureth all things.

Charity never faileth: but whether there be prophecies, they shall fail; whether there be tongues, they shall cease; whether there be knowledge, it shall vanish away.

For we know in part, and we prophesy in part.

But when that which is perfect is come, then that which is in part shall be done away. When I was a child I spake as a child, I understood as a child, I thought as a child; but when I became a man, I put away childish things.

For now we see through a glass darkly; but then face to face: now I know in part; but then shall I know even as also I am known.

And now abideth faith, hope, charity, these three; but the greatest of these is charity.

## *The Address*

We are gathered here to celebrate a marriage, a spiritual union that embodies love's most profound possibilities. Saint Paul, the author of this letter to the Corinthians, uses the word *charity* to refer to the highest form of love that we can ever ask of ourselves. As we have heard in these readings, love in this form is the greatest of virtues; love is the highest spiritual work. Love is both immanent and transcendent. And it is love, kindled by romance and clasped by heartfelt marriage vows, that has the capacity to deliver marriage from being merely a domestic arrangement, a supportive partnership, and an emotional bonding, and elevate it into a spiritual enterprise.

To speak of marriage as a spiritual enterprise is to view it in a slightly different way than normally, and certainly not simply in a romantic light. For when we speak of marriage in spiritual terms, we are inviting ourselves into it—and it into us—at a much higher level. To participate in a marriage of this kind is not only to enter into it as the estate that will bring us happiness, but to see it also as the spiritual crucible of transformation, of suffering, and also of great joy.

Therefore, as you step into marriage you must remember first of all that marriage is a process of transformation. Because of it, inside of it, and in response to it, you will change most remarkably. And not necessarily or exclusively in the ways you had hoped for or imagined. For marriage is the spiritual grinding stone that will hone you to your brightest brilliance. It will cause you to become not only who you wanted to be, but also the person whom you have no choice but to be. In marriage you will be re-formed, for in choosing this particular person to love and make your whole life with, you are choosing to be affected. You will be polished through the actions of your beloved upon you, through the praise, criticism, frustration, excitement, actions, and inactions of the person you marry today.

In this regard it is important to remember that, more than you can possibly imagine, you are unconsciously drawn to precisely that person who possesses the attributes you need to be affected by in order to change. These are the very qualities which, because of their capacity to irritate and inspire you, will encourage in you the very dimensions you lack, the qualities which, as you acquire them, will represent an enlargement of your soul. What this means, simply, is that in spite of yourself you will be drawn into a process of personal evolution. Whatever is missing in your character will gradually be developed and what's remarkable about this transformation is that in the end, rather than feeling bitter, resentful, or unwilling, you will come to see the acquisition of these attributes as an exquisite refinement of your spirit.

This is a spiritual process because it deals not with the superficial aspects of your personality, how you dress and what you eat—although changes in these areas may also be part of the process—but with the deepest essence of your being and, ultimately, with your capacity to love. You will learn to be kinder, or more gently critical, to be empathetic, or more trusting. For wherever we are bound by our own emotional limitations, wherever we have judgments, or cannot come into the presence of our own generosity or compassion because of our woundedness, there certainly, we will be met in marriage. We will be met in the character of our beloved, with an invitation to transcend our own limitations—our judgments, our stinginess, our lack of trust, our fear of intimacy, our pride, our self-focus, our self-righteousness, and strive for their beautiful opposites, to reach, in short, for our capacity to love.

For it is love, of course, true love, unconditional love, the love of the tree for the earth, the love of the bird for the air, the love of God for creation, which shatters all limitations, which dissolves all fears. This unconditional love is the true gift of marriage, its greatest, most spirit-embracing work.

As marriage will change us and develop in us the true power of our love, so also will it call us to the highest labors of that love. First Corinthians 13, for example, talks about the specific qualities of love that allow us to develop as spirits. It tells us that along with bearing, believing, hoping, and enduring, "love suffers long." So we are being instructed through this ancient writing that love isn't only the roses and romance that bring us to the altar, but that it includes, more formidably, the quality Saint Paul calls "suffering." This sounds difficult, certainly not something that would entice us into marriage; so what, exactly, do we mean by suffering?

Among its many meanings are: "to undergo, to experience, to pass through, to endure without sinking . . . to allow, to permit, to not forbid or hinder"; also, "to tolerate, to put up with."

Thus, when Corinthians says that love suffers long, it does not mean that love is masochistic or foolish, but that love is generous, brave, creative, enduring, adventurous, and strong.

Through such contemplation, we are

being invited to move beyond the romantic view of marriage and encounter the truth that in marriage love does, indeed, "suffer" in all these meanings of the word—and to a most remarkable degree. For it is in the nature of love to participate, to undergo—and not as an exception, but as the rule. Love calls upon us, not only for the sake of our beloved but also in the service of love itself, to constantly expand our reach, to become much more than we are.

Thus in what we will bear, go through, endure without sinking, or just plain put up with, marriage encourages us to the ultimate expansion of our capabilities. It is in this way that love invites us into the state of spiritual evolution which requires that, on behalf of our beloved, we pass again and again through what we believe are our own limitations, that over and over we accept the seemingly unacceptable and endure what we believe we cannot endure.

To know that marriage has a high spiritual purpose is to be willing to bear the sufferings that lie along its path. But it is also to rejoice and be glad, to be exuberant and playful, to bask in the companionship of the person who delights you, to participate in the joys of incarnation by being happy animals, creatures of passion and habit and comfort.

For marriage as a spiritual enterprise is also, in essence, about joy. It is joy that brings us to marriage, joy that inhabits its happiest moments, and joy with which we shall contemplate it when our lives draw to a close. For it is the joy of all joy, the infinite joy, which in its finite form a marriage symbolizes. For joy, unlike happiness, which is merely an emotion, is a state of being—that state of ultimate bliss and intimate union in which nothing and no one is separate from anything or anyone. In joy are we born; to joy we shall return. Joy is an endless ecstatic state, the ultimate spiritual condition.

To suffer the challenges of marriage is also to deliver yourself to its joys—to joy itself. And it is thus, in the spirit of joy, that we welcome____ and ____ to the spiritual undertaking that is marriage. Long may it stand as the cathedral of their love.

## *The Consecration*

Dear God, look mercifully upon your children, _____ and _____, and be generous with them so that in the unfolding veils of time, they may truly stand for one another as emblems of the incarnation of your love. Give them a sense of joy, of excitement, of possibility, and challenge about what they are undertaking here, the ever-unfolding and beautiful work of refining their spirits in the presence of each other's witness, of becoming the bearers of your love.

And knowing that this is a high and often difficult work, that its rewards are uncommon, invisible, often, in ordinary day to day life, we pray for them the benediction of company, the encouragement of witnesses, the boundless joy of living always in the midst of love.

Give them peace of heart and strength of spirit so they may honor the vows they make here today. And may the promises they make inspire and instruct each one of us who celebrates with them. Amen.

## *The Expression of Intent*

Now that you have heard the high calling of marriage, do you _____ choose _____ to be your honored and cherished wife (husband/partner/mate), to live with her (him) and love her (him) in the consecrated state of marriage?

Answer: I do choose to marry her (him).

## *The Vows*

In the name of God, I, ___, take you, ___, to be my beloved wife (husband/mate),
to have you and hold you,
to honor you, to treasure you
to be at your side in sorrow and in joy
to suffer with you and to be transformed,
and to love and cherish you always.

I promise you this from my heart, with my soul
for all the days of my life
and if God wills
beyond the walls of life
beyond the bounds of time.

### The Blessing of the Rings

As God is a circle whose center is everywhere and whose circumference is nowhere, so let the seamless circle of these rings become the symbol of your endless love.

### The Exchanging of the Rings

Beloved ____, I give you this ring
as a symbol of my steadfastness and joy
in loving you, and as a pledge to honor you
with all that I am and all I shall become
for my whole life.

### The Pronouncement of Marriage

Now that you, ____, and you, ____, have prom-ised to give yourselves to one another and to love each other through your sacred vows and through the giving and receiving of these rings, I now pronounce you husband and wife (married).

Those whom God has joined together may he generously bless forever. You may now kiss one another.

## *The Kiss*

## *The Benediction*

Because you can rest in the comfort of knowing that you are chosen through one another to serve the highest purposes of love, depart in peace, recognizing that what you undertake together will bring you inestimable joy, and that the love you share can truly help to change the world. Now go forth from this place with jubilation in your hearts and gladness in your feet. Amen.

# The Marriage
# of Love and Purpose

*T*his ceremony sees marriage as a celebration of human destiny. It acknowledges that the union will have as one of its major commitments the willingness of the partners to search for, discover, and support one another as they step into the presence of what is theirs, truly, to do in this life.

Couples who are drawn to this ceremony are those to whom their own psychological development and emotional healing are of paramount importance in their lives. They have a sense of destiny, indeed a sense of urgency, about discovering who they are and what, in some ultimate sense, their lives are about.

Of course we don't all always consciously know the direction our lives are taking, or how the person to whom we are attracted fits in to this process. We may know simply that we have fallen in love and find ourselves getting married. Even if your purposes are not as clear to you as you might imagine they could be from the words of this wedding, but you are open to discovering them, this ceremony is one you will want to consider.

Some people have already set themselves on the path of discovering what their life purpose is, and they see their beloved as being as intricately related to the fulfillment of their own destiny as they are to the fulfillment of their partner's. If you are a couple who operate from this perspective, you have already been asking yourselves a lot of questions about who you are and what you intend to do with your life. You have already made knowing yourselves a high priority. In keeping with these values, as you contemplate the celebration of your wedding, you will want to consider carefully what it is that you wish to say and have said at this, the ceremonial portal to the fulfillment of your common and individual purposes.

Therefore, you will want to ask yourself

not only what you desire to receive from your union in support of your own destiny but also what the two of you together, in the particular and unique configuration of your marriage, have been brought together to accomplish. What is your own personal destiny? What is your common life about? What, through your union, can you develop and nurture in one another? Where, in the present and the long future, do you as a couple mean to go? How can you go there beautifully and what part does your partner play in the process of your mutual and individual unfolding?

Asking and answering these questions as you plan your wedding will allow you to create a ceremony that truly reflects the highest values you hold for your lives. Then, just as the arrow strung in the bow is already poised for its highest destination, so your wedding ceremony shall become the moment in which you set the loftiest purposes of your life in motion.

## *The Convocation*

____ and ____, Mr. and Mrs. (names of the bride's parents), Mr. and Mrs. ____ (names of the groom's parents), beloved friends, colleagues, accomplices, witnesses, we have come here to celebrate the marriage and the intertwining of the destinies of ____ and ____, who, through being ruthlessly and wonderfully themselves, have fallen in love and chosen to get married.

Whether we know it or not the path of our lives is already laid out deep within us, and life is the process of being willing to discover the direction of our path, the giving of ourselves to whatever it takes to be able to hit the mark. In other words, we are all here for a reason, and it is our business, as our lives progress, not only to discover what that purpose is but also to cultivate the conditions—whether emotional, educational, personal, or geographic—that allow us to fulfill that highest purpose.

In this context, marriage is a nurturing

matrix in which two individuals can continue to expand and develop, so they can fulfill their individual destinies and offer their gifts to life and to the world. In this view, the focus is not so much on the couple and what they may undertake together, but more on the power of the individuals and what they have to contribute through their lives, how their union serves to enlarge and develop each of them.

While this may appear on the surface to be an unromantic vision of love, it is a view that holds a relationship in the highest spiritual regard, for it has as its underlying assumption that each of us is alive for an important purpose and that marriage enhances that capacity for individual contribution and participation.

_____ and _____ have stretched their individual development so far that they are no longer laboring alone to become themselves, but have arrived at the point in self-discovery where they can offer themselves as accomplices of destiny to one another.

It is in this spirit that they marry, not just

because of their ineffable attraction to one another, but because the composite of their experiences has brought them to the place where they are ready to fulfill what is theirs to accomplish in this life, to join the forces of their individual spirits, capabilities, and backgrounds for the purpose of accomplishing together and individually what is theirs to do.

Therefore we celebrate with them their arrival at the portal of true and conscious loving. We are incredibly happy for them and with them that one of the landmarks in the vast landscape of their becoming is the love that has brought them, and us, to the joyous occasion of this marriage.

## *The Invocation*

All-knowing spirit in whose presence all human spirits bend to their becoming, we invite, indeed we entreat, you to join us in this ceremony binding the lives and destinies of \_\_\_\_ and \_\_\_\_. As they speak and we hear the words that will they speak and we hear the words that will forever join them, allow the intentions being uttered in their hallowed conversation to stand true in time and run deep as a singing river through the landscape of their lives.

## The Readings

### In Love Made Visible

In love are we made visible
As in a magic bath
are unpeeled
to the sharp pit
so long concealed

With love's alertness
we recognize
the soundless whimper
of the soul
behind the eyes
A shaft opens
and the timid thing
at last leaps to surface
with full-spread wing

The fingertips of love discover
more than the body's smoothness
They uncover a hidden conduit
for the transfusion
of empathies that circumvent
the mind's intrusion

In love are we set free
Objective bone
and flesh no longer insulate us
to ourselves alone
We are released
and flow into each other's cup
Our two frail vials pierced
drink each other up

*May Swenson*

# A Vision

Two angels among the throng of angels
paused in the upward abyss,
facing angel to angel.

Blue and green glowed the wingfeathers
of one angel, from red to gold the sheen
of the other's. These two,

so far as angels may dispute, were poised
on the brink of dispute, brink of
fall from angelic stature,

for these tall ones, angels
whose wingspan encompasses entire
earthly villages, whose heads if their feet touched
            earth

would top pines or redwoods, live by their
            vision's harmony
which sees at one glance
the dark and light of the moon.

These two hovered dazed before one another,
for one saw the seafeathered, peacock breakered
crests of the other angel's magnificence,
different from his own,

and the other's eyes flickered with vision of
flame petallings, cream-gold grainfeather glitter
       ings,
the wings of his fellow,
and both in immortal danger of dwindling, of
       dropping
into the remote forms of a lesser being.

But as these angels, the only halted ones
among the many who passed and repassed,
trod air as swimmers tread water, each gazing

on the angelic wings of the other,
the intelligence proper to great angels flew into
       their wings,
the intelligence called intellectual love, which,
understanding the perfections of scarlet,

leapt up among blues and greens strongshafted,
and among amber down illumined the sapphire
      bloom,

so that each angel was iridescent with the strange
      newly-seen
hues he watched; and their discovering pause
and the speech their silent interchange of perfec-
      tion was

never became a shrinking to opposites,

and they remained free in the heavenly chasm,
remained angels, but dreaming angels,
each imbued with the mysteries of the other.
                *Denise Levertov*

# The Address

____ and ____, you are here because separately and for a long time, you have each chosen the path of self-knowledge. You have paid attention to who you are, what your life means, and where you are going. But today, this day of your wedding, is the occasion of the shedding your solitary journeys in favor of bonding yourself with one another; and your marriage, as well as being the estate of joining with another human being, is also the union of two people committed to the process of their own becoming.

Since you have always attended to your individual selves, to the process of understanding yourselves, healing your own emotional wounds, and learning to be faithful to your prodigious talents, marriage is more than a merging, a blending, or the melting together of the two of you. Rather, it is the ascension of two stately trees growing tall side by side in the forest; it is two angels recognizing one another at the edge of the abyss.

For you marriage is neither absorption nor displacement. Neither of you hopes for, nor would you tolerate, your own disappearance. To be "lost in love" is not your desire; to be subsumed by attachment to someone else's identity is not your image of yourself; to be somebody's "better"—or lesser—half is unthinkable. What you desire and what you require from marriage is somehow different than what is conjured by the usual picture of character-homogenizing wedded bliss. You desire above all the marriage of your true selves, you insist that your marriage be an environment in which as individual beings you can flourish.

Because you believe this so sincerely, because union with individual freedom is what you hope for and intend, there are a number of things which, as you step across the drawbridge to the castle of marriage, you need to hold fast to.

First, remember to honor your individual selves, to keep hold of the vision of your individual destinies. This is what you have labored to create; your selves are your greatest treasure, what, in fact, you are each here to share with one another. But while in the past you were able to remember and focus on your journey in a solitary context, now you must be yourself in conjunction with another, and keeping track of your destiny in the midst of a marriage is quite another matter. It's harder; the thrills and demands of the union will distract and charm you and perhaps entice you off your path. But no matter how beautiful or captivating your marriage may be, your relationship as itself can never stand in the place of, nor do service for, what you as individuals came here to accomplish.

In this sense, marriage is the handmaiden of the individuals in it, the supportive context that nourishes the possibilities alive within you. The challenge in marriage is to continue to expand and grow, to honor the full stature of one another, to support the impending expansion that lies within you. Thus, even when you are tempted to dwindle down to the most minimal definition of what being married can be, seeing yourselves only—or first and foremost—as a couple, resist that temptation. Remember that your relationship is a source, the fountain of nourishment for who you both are individually.

Second, remember that your relationship, as itself, has a destiny, and that your marriage is a living, striving organism. It has a nature and attributes of its own that are distinct from, and larger and more intricate than, the characteristics of the individuals who comprise it.

A relationship has its own mysterious sense of balance, its own timing, its unique choreography, its particular destination. It will carry you along with it to where it needs to go, but if you are overly focused on the *me* and the *I* of yourselves, the relationship itself, that mysterious magical animal, may become starved and lie down like a tired old dog at the side of the road.

So be kind to your relationship. Treat it with respect and nourish it with the entertainments, diversions, purposes, mementos, and happy anticipations it needs to keep it young and puppy-like.

And finally, while you are sailing your little boat on the great sea of marriage, take care as you navigate to avoid being dashed up on either the Sylla of ignoring yourselves or the Charybdis of ignoring the relationship itself; remember to remember love.

For it is love, after all and before all, that has brought you to this place. Love is the inspiration, the magic, and the healing balm of any marriage, no matter how clearly envisioned or powerfully determined its destiny may be. Love is what brought you together; love is what will keep you whole. And so, as you tend to the endless and spirit-unraveling requirements of what your individual destinies will inevitably demand, return in your hearts again and again to the love between you. Love will delight you. Love will most happily distract you when you are tempted to become too serious, too heavy-handed, or overly involved in all your own important undertakings. Love will give you joy. Love will give meaning to the pursuit of your destinies. For love is life's highest destiny, its greatest purpose, and its finest work.

## *The Consecration*

Seeing that no moment is without meaning, no undertaking is without significance, no individual is of such quality as to be diminished by even so important an enterprise as marriage, we ask that you both, together and as your irreplaceably special selves, be honored and expanded by the promises you are about to make, the marriage you are about to create. And may love, that destiny above all destinies, be always in your midst, the handmaid and the master of your marriage.

## *The Expression of Intent*

Having been reminded once again of the deep value of your own self knowing, and understanding that marriage is the convergence of your individual and joint destinies as well as the greatest support for them, that as well as being a mirror for the study of yourselves, your marriage is in itself a worthy enterprise, do you, ____, choose to marry ____, to speak the words that will bind you to her (him) as her husband (his wife) and allow you to become most fully yourself in her (his) presence for the rest of the days of your life?

   Answer: I do.

## *The Vows*

Dearest ____,
I do now choose you and take you
to be my wife (husband/partner/mate),
to witness and assist in my becoming,
to hold me, as your beloved, in your heart.

I give you my love, the steadfastness
of my purpose, my will, and my hope,
and my highest intention that always,
in one another's presence,
we may unflinchingly become who we are,
and with unswerving commitment
be willing to do what we came here to do.

You are my lover, my teacher, my model,
my accomplice, and my true counterpart.
I will love you, hold you, and honor you,
respect you, encourage you, and cherish you,
in health and in sickness
through sorrow and success
for all the days of my life.

## The Blessing of the Rings

Rings are made precious by our wearing of them.
They carry our meaning; they say who we are,
where we have been, and where we are going.
They become us; they reflect us; they are a
symbol of our truest essence.

      Your wedding rings are most special
because they say that even in your uniqueness
you have chosen to be bonded, to allow the
presence of another human being to enhance
who you are. Your rings carry the potent double
message: we are individuals and yet we belong;
we are not alone. As you wear them through

time, they will reflect not only who you are but also the union you are making, the fact that through the rest of your lives each of you will be imprinted by the other, yet as yourself remain.

## The Exchanging of the Rings

As a sign of my love
and that I am choosing
to share my whole life's journey
with you, and of my knowing that in marrying
you I shall become much more than I am,
I give you this ring, with the pledge
that through you, I shall be most truly myself
and offer such gifts as I have
and I am to the world.

## The Pronouncement of Marriage

Now having freely chosen to leave behind the private vigil of seeking self-knowledge in solitude, and having taken up the task of clearly seeing and supporting another human being, having promised your love by honoring one another with the gift of your rings, I now pronounce you husband and wife (married).

## *The Kiss*

## *The Benediction*

May all that you have already become, which has brought you to this day, and all you will become as a consequence of it, in the lifelong joining of your hearts and minds, continue to show you your purpose.

May you always be brought most beautifully and steadfastly into the presence of yourselves and of one another, and may you live long and happily fulfilling all that you are. Amen.

# The Marriage of Love and Rejoicing

*T*he mood of this wedding is one of festivity and well-being. You are here to celebrate your wonderful good fortune and the inevitability of it all, how wonderful it is that you two got together and how deliciously right it feels to love one another.

In this ceremony, the point is not so much to emphasize the challenges of marriage as to delight in the pure miraculousness that any two people could so happily find and so joyfully come home to one another.

Love really is something over which we have no control. We can need it, wish for it, long for it, but all on our own, even with rigid self-discipline, we cannot insist it into being. Therefore, when love finds us, when the person we simply can't live without crosses our path, it is truly a gift and the wedding that celebrates this star-fated mating is indeed a happy occasion.

## *The Convocation*

Love is a miraculous gift, and a wedding is a celebration of that magic, and that's what were here to do today. We are gathered together to be overjoyed for and with \_\_\_\_\_ and \_\_\_\_\_ who are so wonderfully suited to one another that it's a pure delight for the rest of us to see how ebulliently happy two people can be.

When we think of love we sometimes talk about people who "deserve" one another. Not only do\_\_\_\_\_ and \_\_\_\_\_ deserve one another, but they are a perfect match, a pair, a fit, two hybrid peas in a pod, and their marriage, far from being something they have had to work hard to achieve, was pure inevitability. They were given to one another, were so star-crossed, and fell so deeply in love that they had no choice.

They are the embodiment of true romance which matured, becomes true love. They are the example of love that in its lightheartedness dissolves the notion of love as hard work. They are the promise of possibility, the expectation of joyful surprise.

So, hooray! We're here to celebrate, to honor, to laugh, to dance, and be glad because the inevitable has happened. Love is alive and well in the land. _____and _____ are here to prove it, and we are here to celebrate with them.

## *The Invocation*

Angels, magicians, wizards, and all good beings, join with us on this happy day and let this be a day of gladness, thanksgiving, possibility, and great good fortune for all of us, but especially for _____ and _____ who are coming together to demonstrate the wonder of love through the celebration of their marriage.

We all live in the hope of loving and being loved, and any sign of the blossoming of love is a true inspiration. Therefore we give thanks for the sweet happiness of _____ and _____. Their enthusiasm is electric, their belief in the destiny of their love is inspiring; their great expectations encourage us beyond measure.

Marriage is a very special place, the

sheltered environment in which we can endlessly explore ourselves in the presence of another and in which we can offer the possibility of the true reflection of another. We are so happy that _____ and _____ have found one another, that they know in their souls how perfectly mated they are, and that they are choosing on this day of most special days to become for all time the accurate and beautiful reflection of each other's essence. We ask that the vision they have of one another be always informed by the spellbinding radiant power that first brought them together, and we pray that as they move into the hallowed ground that is marriage they may always hold one another in the light of all light, the love of all love.

# The Readings

## we are so both and oneful
(last stanza)

we are so both and oneful
night cannot be so sky
sky cannot be so sunful
i am through you so i
*e.e. cummings*

## The Passionate Shepherd to His Love

Come live with me and be my love,
And we will all the pleasures prove
That valleys, groves, hills, and fields,
Woods, or steepy mountain yields.
And we will sit upon the rocks,
Seeing the shepherds feed their flocks,
By shallow rivers to whose falls

Melodious birds sing madrigals.

And I will make thee beds of roses
And a thousand fragrant posies,
A cap of flowers, and a kirtle
Embroidered all with leaves of myrtle;

A gown made of the finest wool
Which from our pretty lambs we pull;
Fair lined slippers for the cold,
With buckles of the purest gold;

A belt of straw and ivy buds,
With coral clasps and amber studs:
And if these pleasures may thee move,
Come live with me, and be my love.

The shepherds' swains shall dance and sing
For thy delight each May morning:
If these delights thy mind may move,
Then live with me and be my love.

*Christopher Marlowe*

## From Sonnets from the Portuguese

How do I love thee? Let me count the ways.
I love thee to the depth and breadth and height
My soul can reach, when feeling out of sight
For the ends of Being and ideal Grace.
I love thee to the level of everyday's
Most quiet need, by sun and candle-light.
I love thee freely, as men strive for Right;
I love thee purely, as they turn from Praise.
I love thee with the passion put to use
In my old griefs, and with my childhood's faith.
I love thee with a love I seemed to lose
With my lost saints—I love thee with the breath,
Smiles, tears, of all my life!—and, if God choose,
I shall but love thee better after death.

*Elizabeth Barrett Browning*

## The Address

We're gathered here today to celebrate the
wedding of ___ and ___, and we are exuberant
and grateful. We're exuberant because, frankly,
it's wonderful that ____ and ____ have fallen in

love, that they feel so good about one another, so delighted, and encouraged, so known and supported, that they've chosen to risk to love for life, to take the great emotional trapeze leap of linking up with one another mid-air and mid-flight. Their optimism is an inspiration; their daring is exhilarating.

For them, of course, today is absolutely wonderful, a magical rabbit pulled out of life's hat. Out of the routine of ordinary life the extraordinary has happened. They didn't have a clue that they would stumble on one another at (include here a bit of where and how you met: the parking garage where she locked her keys in the car, the train station in Venice, his boss' birthday party . . . ), go through all the thrills and frettings of the initial delicious stages of romance, to discover the love of substance and depth they are consecrating with marriage today. They were so happy that they didn't even realize they were serious, that the love that so utterly captivated them, that made them feel like schoolchildren, was also a love of depth and importance. Romance is play, but true love is intention, and it is their intending to love for life that we are celebrating today.

But today is also a celebration for the rest of us, for it is also a pleasure for us to see love in bloom, to participate in the wedding of two people so delightfully suited to one another. It lifts our spirits to be in the presence of such a love, to bask in the sweet energies of two people who so obviously adore one another, who want to play together, laugh together, walk together for a lifetime. Love untarnished, that is the gift that _____ and _____ and give us; love with garlands of ribbons and posies, love with infinite hope.

Therefore, _____ and _____, we thank you. You've brightened our day. Thanks for letting us celebrate with you; thanks for showing us that love can bloom, that marriage is a worthy enterprise, and that happy, high-spirited people are overjoyed to undertake it.

And now, before we get to the party, let me say a few words of encouragement and direction to you two. First of all, a wedding is a happy occasion, flawless in its good humor, its joyful sense of well-being, but your marriage won't

always be like this. For, as you live it out, you will
discover that your relationship has moods and
seasons, high times as well as lulls and dead-dog
bone-dry gulches. From time to time the delightful spirit of this wedding day will not be with
you, and when it is taken over by the love
grinches, you will have to reach for something
deeper in yourselves, for the love that is stronger
than feel-good; the love that is truer than fun, the
love that requires energy as well as feasts on it.

Your wedding is an unmitigatedly happy
occasion, but your marriage will be a many-
textured thing. In it, both magic and sorrows will
befall you. You will intend one thing and end up
doing another. You will imagine your darling to
be a certain way and discover that he is not, that
she is a person unto herself. You will have
clashes and discover things you did and did not
want to know. You will rumple each other's
spirits as well as bedclothes and hair. You will
say mean and terrible words, and, for love, be
able to forget them. You will betray one another
in tiny and sometimes huge and perhaps devas-
tating ways, and, for love, forgive one another

and go on.

These, the great and petty perils of marriage, are an invitation to refine your love and deepen it, to expand it beyond the light-spiritedness and laughter that enliven your hearts today and explore the more profound reaches of compassion, of tender caring, of selfless nurturing. These capacities are the maturing of love through time, love's highest calling and its finest work; and marriage is the summons to be open not only to these challenges but also to the opportunities, unexpected and not necessarily always welcome, that invite them into being.

Second, remember that a relationship is a progression. There's an old Chinese proverb that says: the journey of a thousand miles begins with a single step. For you, ___ and ____, your wedding today is an exquisite and beautifully choreographed first step. With it, you are passing through a portal which will lead you to many places, including ones you can't possibly imagine. Wherever it takes you, there will be surprises, for this is the mark of a truly loving relationship—that it will take you where you had not meant to go.

There is great joy to be found in such a surprising journey, with twists and turns, shades and possibilities beyond your wildest imaginings. Instead of resisting the changes, allow them to flower in you and know that they are leading you somewhere, that separately and together, you are becoming more than you were. Don't expect every day to have the fanciful mood or the exuberant high spirits of this, your wedding day, but be excited, open-minded, curious, available, and inquiring about you are becoming. Know that your composite experiences are turning you into the highest form of yourselves, that you are becoming the best and the most, that you are doing the things which only you two together could possibly do.

Therefore, along with celebrating the marvelous feelings of today, remember, especially when you are saying your vows, that you are also promising to love for the long and ambivalent future. If you can hold onto this intention, then instead of bowing down or bowing out when you've misplaced your delight, you can ride out the storms with confidence, knowing that the thunderhead-clouded skies are temporary and not a reflection of your relationship as a whole.

Above all, remember that love is what matters. Love will prevail. It is the love you feel for one another that will be the answer to all your difficulties. If in marrying you have chosen well and promised wisely, love will be stronger than all the conflicts, bigger than the changes. Love will be the miracle always inviting you to learn, to blossom, to expand. And it is to love—to the love you are celebrating, embodying, and radiating on this special day—that you must return.

So remember these things, my dear ones, as you go out into the world as a couple: that your love will have seasons, that your relationship is a progression, and that love will prevail. Remembering them, holding them in your hearts and in your minds, will give you a marriage that is as deep in its joy as your courtship has been in its magic.

Congratulations, _____ and _____, the real fun has just begun.

## The Consecration

Enfolded in joy, inhabited by hope, bathed in the infinite spectrum of light that is love, may you be always infused with it and beautifully illumined by it.

May every desire you have for your love be fulfilled, and may you be given the vision with which to clearly behold one another, the listening with which to perceive one another most genuinely, and the endless generosity of spirit with which to nourish one another's souls and sweetly keep the promises you make here today.

## The Expression of Intent

_____ and _____, now that you have heard about the magic and the mysteries of marriage, the way it will continuously surprise you, the strength and wisdom it will everlastingly ask of you, do you choose still and happily and in our midst to make the promises of marriage?

Do you _____ want to marry _____, to happily hold her (him) above all and have her (him) as your bride and wife (groom and husband, life partner)?

Answer: I certainly do.

## *The Vows*

From this day on I most choose you, my beloved

\_\_\_\_,

to be my wife (husband/mate/life partner),
to live with you and laugh with you;
to stand by your side and sleep in your arms;
to be joy to your heart and food to your soul;
to bring out the best in you always;
and, for you, to be the most that I can.

To laugh with you in the good times;
to struggle with you in the bad;
to solace you when you are downhearted;
to wipe your tears with my hands;
to comfort you with my body;
to mirror you with my soul;
to share with you all my riches and honors;

to play with you as much as I can
until we grow old, and still loving
each other sweetly and gladly,
our lives shall come to the end.

## The Blessing of the Rings

These rings are made of precious metals, a
symbol of the riches that reside in each of you;
and as any metal is purified by the white heat of
testing, so will your love be purified by the tests
that are given to you through the many seasons
of your loving.

 These rings are made of precious jewels;
and as the elements from which these jewels are
formed are ancient as the stars, as mysterious as
moonlight, and as shining as the miracle of your
new-bonded radiance, wear them as the sign of
the love ignited between you, the love un-
quenchable which now your hearts embody and
your words express.

## The Exchanging of the Rings

Dearest, ____, my love,
this ring is the token of my love
and of the hopes and all the joys
I most dearly behold in you.

You are my promise and my
most magically answered plea,
you are my wish, my dream, my quest;
you are my gift, my lover, my double,
my perfectly matching mate.

You are my light, my love, my limbs,
my soul's most mirroring shadow,
my body's closest friend.

I marry you with this ring, with
the wings of my love, with all
that I have and I am.

Answer:
Thank you, my love.
I will wear forever this ring
as the sign of my joy
and the depth of your love.

## *The Pronouncement of Marriage*

\_\_\_\_ and \_\_\_\_, now that you have heard the words about love and marriage, now that you have shown us the example of your love and celebrated your union by giving each other these beautiful rings, it is with great joy and happiness that I now pronounce you husband and wife (married). You may now kiss.

## *The Kiss*

## *The Benediction*

God bless you, beautiful young ones. May the wings of angels uphold you through all the life of your love, may you live forever in happiness with one another. May your hearts be full; may your lips stay sweet. May your love grow strong; may you love long and happily in one another's arms.

# The Marriage of Love and Fulfillment

*I*f you have been married before you are no doubt approaching this new marriage with feelings that differ markedly from those you had when you were a first-time bride or groom. Subsequent marriages represent commitment in the face of disappointment or loss; celebration tempered by a previous experience of disillusionment. Therefore, in both what you say to one another and what you choose to have said at your ceremony, you will want to acknowledge that as well as celebrating the love you share now, you are remembering the love that wounded you in the past.

Sometimes this wounding was betrayal, a trust that was broken, sometimes the unbearable sorrow of losing a mate to death. As this ceremony is primarily geared to those previously divorced, if you are a widow or widower marrying again, you may want to tailor this ceremony a little more precisely to your needs.

When it comes to losses—in life and in love—we all tend to want to let bygones be bygones, to shove our mistakes and disheartenments under the rug. Of course it's nice, if you can, to put your troubles out of your mind. But if you want this marriage to be a success, and if you want this wedding to catapult you into the relationship that really will last the rest of your life, don't try to bury the truth about your past. Instead, let the uniqueness of this wedding celebration arise precisely from the fact that it stands in counter-point to a marriage or marriages which for one reason or another came to an end. Be bold in celebrating your hopes and in enlisting the support of your friends, as you have the courage, once again—and differently—to make your marriage vows.

## *The Convocation*

We have come here together today to celebrate the marriage and reflect the incredible joy of ____ and ____, who, after several dress rehearsals and detours (or, after almost overwhelming losses), long after they believed that it was possible, have been given the great good fortune of falling in love with one another.

A wedding is the celebration of the miracle of love, and that's what we're here to do: to celebrate that miracles do occur, that at any moment, the unexpected can happen; and that after almost giving up hope, most inexplicably and wonderfully, the path of our entire lives can change.

Marriage is a meditation on our histories as well as on our future, on our losses and failures, as well as our hopes and possibilities. And so, as ____ and ____ wed, it is worthwhile to contemplate that they could not and would not be standing before us today if they had not followed their own star home and done what they needed to do to deliver themselves to this point in their lives.

_____ and _____, you give us hope, and we are overjoyed to be your witnesses. You are the living embodiment of the truth that practice does indeed make perfect, that persistence does, in fact, pay off. We are touched by your happiness; we are moved by the exquisite courage of your love. It gives us incomparable joy to celebrate with you, to be reminded that true love, abiding love, is the consequence of the practice of love, and that nothing we do in this life is ever wasted or lost.

## *The Invocation*

God, the great magician, you leave us spellbound with your generosity. In bringing ____ and _____ together, you invite us to comprehend that love is a profound and mysterious process, and that because of--and in spite of—those with whom we have shared our lives in the past, we have been ineluctably shaped as ourselves. In delivering ____ and ____ to this place, you teach us to comprehend that love is a process. It is the unfolding, honing, grinding, and preparing of ourselves that enables us to stand in the presence of another human being and embrace that person with the love we have been waiting a whole lifetime to experience.

We thank you for this miraculous day, for the fulfillment of love we see before us, and for the joy of sharing this happy occasion.

## *The Readings*

## *The Ivy Crown*

The whole process is a lie,
      unless,
            crowned by excess,
it break forcefully,
        one way or another,
           from its confinement--
or find a deeper well.
        Anthony and Cleopatra
                were right;
they have shown
        the way.  I love you
           or I do not live
at all.
Daffodil time
        is past.  This is
           summer, summer!
the heart says,
        and not even the full of it.
           No doubts
are permitted—

though they will come
and may
before our time
overwhelm us.
We are only mortal
but being mortal
can defy our fate.
We may
by an outside chance
even win! We do not
look to see
jonquils and violets
come again
but there are,
still,
the roses!

Romance has no part in it.
The business of love is
cruelty which,
by our wills,
we transform
to live together.
It has its seasons,

for and against,
    whatever the heart
fumbles in the dark
    to assert
        toward the end of May.
Just as the nature of briars
    is to tear flesh,
        I have proceeded
through them.
    Keep
        the briars out,
they say.
    You cannot live
        and keep free of
briars.
Children pick flowers.
    Let them.
        Though having them
in hand
    they have no further use for them
        but leave them crumpled
at the curb's edge.

At our age the imagination

across the sorry facts
        lifts us
to make roses
        stand before thorns.
                Sure
love is cruel
        and selfish
                and totally obtuse—
at least, blinded by the light,
        young love is.
                But we are older,
I to love
        and you to be loved,
                we have,
no matter how,
        by our wills survived
                to keep
the jeweled prize
        always
                at our finger tips.
We will it so
        and so it is
                past all accident.

*William Carlos Williams*

## *The Address*

Marriage is a bonding of strangers made beautifully familiar through the miracle of love, the process of unstrangering one another through the power of loving and the gift of time. Marriage brings two people together not only in the present, but in the presence of their past, of the lives they have led—the choices they have made, the lessons that have shaped and reshaped the chambers of their hearts. Thus to be marrying again is different than simply to be marrying.

And so, as you contemplate reentering the very state that wounded you, you may be tempted to blind yourself to all the sorrows, difficulties, and disappointments of your past relationships, to look at this marriage as separate, distinct, and completely unrelated to all the relationships that preceded it.

This is a worthy temptation; it would be wonderful to think that this relationship—and your readiness for it—arrived at your doorstep out of the blue. But that isn't the case, and in trying to view it this way you separate yourself from the lessons that brought you here, indeed from your own evolution as a person. For the other relationships you've had, you went through not *instead* of being in this relationship, but *in order* to be in it. This marriage is the culmination of years of apprenticeship, the winnowing and honing of your previous relationships to help shape you into the person who stands here today, ready to make the ultimate commitment of love.

Therefore, when you doubt the relevance of your past—and you will at times—or when you feel embarrassed about it—which, at times you may—remember that every relationship you have had was a step on the path to this relationship. The past was prologue. Every single conflict and disappointment, every beautiful, grueling, and painfully instructive moment in each of those relationships was delivered to your consciousness in preparation for this love.

Your experiences then are the laundry ticket for the silk garments you are retrieving from the cleaners now. What you did then was the antecedent, the exquisitely appropriate conditioning for what you are doing now. Everything was of value; everything taught you something, prepared you for marrying again, most happily now.

Acknowledging the past as preparation allows you to step most gracefully into the present, and having done so, you need to remind one another that this union is unique. This is not just "another" relationship; it is the relationship which is the consequence and fulfillment of the others; it is the last and the best. It has qualities contributed by both of you that make it the highest expression of what you two can offer through the medium of an intimate relationship. Therefore, be generous in reminding one another not only of what a gem of a relationship you have here, but also of the singular set of qualities you each possess—the attributes, values, and convictions—that can allow you to legitimately believe to the depths of your hearts that this is the love that will last until the end of your days.

Sometimes when we've finally arrived at a longed-for destination, there's a temptation simply to be where we are, without discovering the possibilities inherent in our new state. This marriage may feel like a destination, a sweet safe place in which you can finally rest, but it is also an opportunity, the emotional and spiritual environment in which you can both develop to your highest brilliance. This is the person with whom you can do all the precious things you've wanted all your life to do. This is the time to receive and intend, to fulfill not only the joy of your heart but the possibilities of your life.

Therefore, remember to do the simple and beautiful things that will make this love a treasure. Fight well. Play. Communicate with one another. Focus on what you want, and entice your intentions into being. Plan for the things that are important to you: make sure you do them. This love is to be nurtured, to be lived out to the fullest in every aspect of its dreams—in the simple ceremonies of shared daily life, in realized hopes and long-deferred plans, in a quality of emotional exchange and spiritual communion toward which the whole of your life has been leaning.

And finally, be thankful for one another. Love is always a gift. A great compliment is being paid to you in being given another chance, another opportunity to love. You have been delivered to your ultimate partner, the person with whom you can share the fruits of all the lessons in your life. Not everyone has this opportunity; not everyone is granted this cornucopia of happiness.

This love was completely unexpected, the joyful consequence of nothing you could control. While everything you have experienced prepared you for it, there was nothing you could do to actually bring it into being; and so it is, indeed, one of life's totally unexpected miracles.

In the presence of a miracle, one of the great human impulses is to disbelieve it or think that somehow we are unworthy of it. Yet it is in the very nature of miracles that we *are* unworthy of them, that we ourselves did nothing to bring them about. The way to be worthy of the miracle of this love is, simply, to receive it. Open your heart; open your hands, open your eyes, and allow the radiance of this love, this love for which you have waited so long, for which you have learned so much, to utterly and endlessly illumine you.

Love is the gift that has been given to you and it is also the gift that you must now give back: to embody, to live out the love, the hope, the joy, the incomparable radiance, and the incredible mirroring that you have had the great good fortune to be given.

## *The Consecration*

Now that you, ____ and ____ have heard about the path of relationship and can rest in the expectation that the love you have found is the fulfillment of the loves you have lost, we ask that your hearts remain always open with thanksgiving for the miracle that has befallen you, for such happiness ofttimes does not occur. Also, may the promises you make to one another be lived out to the end of your days in an atmosphere of the profoundest joy.

## *The Expression of Intent*

____, Knowing that your heart has been bruised, that the path of marriage has not always brought you joy, that because of your sorrows you have doubted your wisdom and the wholeness of the self that did the choosing, do you choose now, with fresh joy and new love, to marry ____ for the long unfurling future, and for the ever-remaining seasons of your life?

Answer: I do.

## *The Vows*

\_\_\_ , my beloved,
emptying my heart of all others,
I fill it now with you,
to love you until the end of my days
as my most treasured wife (husband/spouse/
       mate).

Remembering the sorrows that have brought me
to this place, acknowledging the lessons I have
       learned,
I set them all aside, and make my life with you.

I will love you, hold you, and honor you
in good times and in bad,
enjoy you, console you, delight you,
astound you when I can,
give thanks for you always,
and cherish you dearly
until the end of our days.

## *The Blessing of the Rings*

Rings are objects of adornment, and while, in a single lifetime, we may have many objects of adornment, we have among them always the one that is most precious to us. May these rings, from this day forward, be your most treasured adornment and may the love they symbolize be, to the end of your days, your most precious possession.

## *The Exchanging of the Rings*

This ring is my thanksgiving,
my promise that I will always love you,
that I will always cherish you
and honor you for all the days of my life.

## The Pronouncement of Marriage

With the sense of incomparable joy that you have found emotional sanctuary for your heart, that you have discovered your life's true love, I now pronounce you husband and wife (married). You may now seal your marriage with a kiss.

## The Kiss

## The Benediction

May you live out your days in joy; may you live in one another's company in peace; may your days be filled with the rewards of all you have endured to bring you to this place. May you endlessly delight one another and may you love and fulfill one another always.

# The Marriage of Love and Renewal

*A*ny marriage is a wonderful occasion, the formal expression of love for two people who are solemnizing their bonds of affection with marriage vows. But for persons who are recovering from an addiction of any kind, marriage is often the highest reward of having finally come to love themselves in a way that for so long they believed impossible.

As anyone who has undergone or is undergoing the process of healing from an addiction will know, a relationship is one of the things you must set aside in order to accomplish your own healing. In this sense, in the initial stages of recovery, solitude is one of the prices you pay for the possibility of redeeming and renewing your life. Later on, however, a relationship becomes the fulfillment of what you have undertaken in the bravery of solitude, the happy consequence of the painstaking process of personal healing.

Because your recovery is the other most important thing in your life and because you have deep feelings about it, you may want your wedding to be an occasion for opening your heart to your sense of gratitude for the new life given you through your recovery process.

The point of view of The Marriage of Love and Renewal is that, rather than holding this truth in abeyance, treating it like a shameful secret you want kept to yourself or hidden between the lines, you are choosing not only to reveal it but to have your recovery itself be acknowledged as a reason for celebration. Not only are you getting married, but you are overjoyed that you are no longer walking through life with the albatross of addiction hanging around your neck. Rather than keeping this truth in the background, you want to bring it forward, making it if not the primary focus, then at least certainly a matter worthy of mention in the course of your wedding ceremony.

I would strongly encourage you to do this.

All too often we treat the sorrows, losses, and difficulties that have most shaped our lives like ugly stepchildren who should be kept out of sight, sweeping up the ashes at the hearth. In truth, it is in our transcendence of them that we become most truly ourselves, and in openly acknowledging them we not only gain a sense of our power over them but also discover a great measure of thanksgiving for the miracle of our survival.

No occasion could be more perfect to acknowledge such beautiful victories than a wedding, and if you are a person who carries one of these spiritual achievements in your bag of tricks, you may want to consider the following ceremony as the appropriate vehicle for expressing your most precious feelings about the life you have left and the new life that awaits you in marriage. Let this be an opportunity to acknowledge, not only to your beloved but to all the people celebrating with you, that indeed you have rejoined the living and that your marriage represents the highest reward of your personal transformation.

## The Convocation

We have come together with great happiness to acknowledge the new life and the emotional delight of ____ and ____, who after struggling with enemies without and within have become the happy and grateful recipients of a deep and abiding love.

A wedding is always a happy occasion, but this one is all the more joyful because it represents not only the coming together of two wonderful people but also the fulfillment of the liberation of their individual selves, the completion of a healing that required great faith and took thousands of intricate steps to accomplish. This is a process with which we can all identify. For while we generally think of recovery as a release from the abuse of a specific substance, all of us struggle against our own personal odds to become most fully ourselves.

We are happy for ____ and ____ and grateful to them because they embody the miracle of the possible. They stand before us revealing the power of love to heal; they teach us that loving yourself is a worthy enterprise; they show us that self-love creates the window of possibility of love between one another.

Their ability to transform their difficulties into new and shining possibilities bodes well for their marriage. For transformation is an unavoidable consequence of marriage, in a sense its greatest achievement; and so as they enter into marriage and even more as they live their lives inside its hallowed gates, rather than resisting the transformations that are the hallmark of love's work, they are already well equipped to embrace the process that will constantly reshape them. They have already shown their willingness to grow beyond their limitations and we join them gladly in the formal solemnizing of their willingness to continue this beautiful process through their marriage.

## *Invocation*

We stand on tiptoe with thanksgiving for the love that has united ____ and ____, the visible reward of their healing and the consecration of their individual lives. We ask that this day be a true celebration not only for them but also for us. Allow us to be inspired by the example of their healing, enlarged by their joy, and delighted by the happiness they have brought into our midst. We give thanks for this beautiful day, for this marvelous occasion, and for the love which is the bond that binds them each to one another and to all of us.

# The Readings

## Ecclesiastes 4: 9-12

Two are better than one, because they have a good reward for their toil. For if they fall, one will lift up his fellow; but woe to him who is alone when he falls and has not another to lift him up. Again, if two lie together, they are warm; but how can one be warm alone? And though a man might prevail against one who is alone, two will withstand him.

## Colossians 3, 12-14

As therefore, God's picked representatives of the new humanity, purified and beloved of God himself, be merciful in action, kindly in heart, humble in mind. Accept life, and be most patient and tolerant with one another, always ready to forgive if you have a difference with anyone. Forgive as freely as the Lord has forgiven you. And, above all, be truly loving, for love is the golden chain of all the virtues.

# To Althea, from Prison
### (last stanza)

Stone walls do not a prison make,
  Nor iron bars a cage;
  Minds innocent and quiet take
  That for an hermitage.
  If I have freedom in my love,
  And in my soul am free,
  Angels alone, that soar above,
  Enjoy such liberty.
                    *Richard Lovelace*

### *somewhere i have never travelled*

somewhere i have never travelled,gladly beyond
any experience,your eyes have their silence:
in your most frail gesture are things which en-
        close me,
or which i cannot touch because they are too
            near

your slightest look easily will unclose me
though i have closed myself as fingers,
you open always petal by petal myself as Spring
        opens
(touching skilfully,mysteriously)her first rose

or if your wish be to close me,i and
my life will shut very beautifully,suddenly,
as when the heart of this flower imagines
the snow carefully everywhere descending;

nothing which we are to perceive in this world
        equals
the power of your intense fragility:whose texture

compels me with the colour of its countries,
rendering death and forever with each breathing

(i do not know what it is about you that closes
and opens;only something in me understands
the voice of your eyes is deeper than all roses)
nobody,not even the rain,has such small hands

*e.e. cummings*

## The Address

There are prisons of the heart and mind, cages in which we lock up our emotions and incarcerate our spirits, which limit our possibilities and are more devastatingly disrupting to our lives than any concrete limitations that can be imposed upon us from the outside. Habits, practices, and substances through which we disown ourselves are among the worst dungeons we can create, and the climb back to light from such darknesses requires that we walk through the pain of all we have tried to erase through anaesthetizing ourselves. That journey is a most demanding and heroic one, one that makes walking down the aisle look like a hop, skip and a jump through a daisy-dappled meadow.

It may seem odd to mention the recovery from an addiction at a wedding, but to ____ and/(or) ____, the deliverance from this bondage was the most important undertaking of her (and/or his) life, a movement from the darkness of annihilation to the bright day of new life, and it is from this happy ground that their love springs.

Love is the ultimate consequence of any process of self-healing, and marriage, living in the presence of another human being as your whole and liberated self, is one of its happiest consequences. Because of your hard work and steadfast commitment, you have each been given one of life's greatest gifts, the opportunity to live in the presence of another human being while discovering your own capacity to bloom.

Just as the recovery from an addiction seeks no reward but itself, so marriage seeks no reward but itself: the simple ineffable joys of living the days of your life with a person who has been given to cherish you.

Therefore on this happy occasion, let us consider certain things. First of all, as you enter into your marriage, remember where you came from. By this I mean that as you proceed on your way, on the emotional merry-go-round of marriage with its unsettlements that can discombobulate you and delights that can equally overwhelm you, remember where you have come from. That is, remember that you weren't always happy and in love. Remember that you were someone who glimpsed the pit of hell in your own particular fashion, and that hell is indeed a real place.

Remember the look of the sky when you could only see it through the bars of the narrow prison window, when you were shut inside the jail of your own making while life continued on the outside, distant and intangible, unattainable to you. Give proper respect to the fact that you, like most of us, were a person who could draw your world so small, that you allowed yourself to be separated from love, from the human community, and from the riches in yourself. Remember the small pinched life you had and the courageous struggle you went through to liberate yourself from it.

Second, after you've remembered who you were and where you've been, forget the monster-infested forests you came from. The very things that are important to remember are also important to forget; and, after taking note of the not-so-happy times in your past, be willing to put them behind you. That's not what your life is about anymore; that's not where you are now.

That's not who you are now. Living is. Loving is.

And finally, after remembering and forgetting where you have been, go where you are going. Marriage is a new phase, and this, the day of your wedding, is the occasion of your joining forces with someone who loves you, just as you are, with all your flaws and possibilities, with all that you have been, and with all that you are becoming. She has her own struggles, her own demons to be fought. He has his own wounds and possibilities, his own, in the words of e.e. cummings, "intense fragility." Staying open to your beloved while remaining true to yourself; treating one another's wounds with tenderness, discovering the power of your gifts and your responsibilities for them, expanding your emotional repertoire to include righteous conflict and the nurturing of your spirits—these are your challenges now.

This is the beginning of a beautiful new chapter of your life. This chapter is vibrant and dramatic; it contains dreams and possibilities, forward movement, action, and endless realizable potentials. You have graduated from the phase of life that you devoted to overcoming something and matriculated into the powerful and wonderful adventure of life as it is now. This chapter is a yes, this chapter is a hurray! This is the coming-out party of all coming-out parties—you as yourself loving someone as him (her) self and believing in a future alive with possibilities.

It is the very act of marrying that creates the possibility of this further transformation. For marriage is more than merely making your life with someone. Marriage is a special kind of sanctuary, a spiritual wing of protection; for in choosing to commit to this degree and to make public your choosing, to submerge and submit your relationship in the midst of the community, you are inviting yourselves to be true to it, not open-endedly, not merely on a whim or as an experiment, but under the canopy of a lifetime promise. In and through this sanctuary, you make to your beloved a lifelong commitment as sacred as the one you have made to yourself, and the future is transformed by your pledge to go "somewhere i have never travelled gladly beyond any experience."

Therefore, \_\_\_ and \_\_\_, with our love and congratulations we set you a-sail in the brave little boat of your marriage, urging you both to remember and forget the difficult landscapes that you have traveled through, always recognizing that love is the ultimate recovery, the happiest destination, and the highest of all rewards. We wish you godspeed on your beautiful journey together.

## *The Consecration*

In the eyes of God, the present is infinitely forever. So let this moment, the apogee of your individual healings, be the present truth that forever eclipses the sorrows of your past. As your lives have opened to the joy of being most wholly and happily yourselves, may you be given the sweetness of heart and the steadfastness of spirit to live in the joy upon joy of loving one another always.

## *The Expression of Intent*

Therefore, _____, after all you have been through,
and after hearing these words about the possibilities and requirements, the rememberings and
forgettings of marriage, do you now choose to
come home to the sanctuary of marriage and
have _____ as your wife (husband/partner/mate)?
      Answer: I do.

## *The Vows*

Because you have witnessed the healing
of my wounds and solaced me in my sorrow,
you have awakened the joy in my heart
and restored well-being to my spirit.
Surely all this goodness can be no mistake,
and is a promise of the miracles to come.
Therefore, I choose you and take you this day
to become my beloved wife (husband/partner/
      mate).

One day at a time, I promise to love you,
to hold you in my heart and with my body,

and, in honor of our love, to steadfastly
pursue the life that makes me whole.

I will support you always in the beautiful
and ever-unfolding process of your healing.
I will honor you in all your undertakings
and stand at your side in times of discourage-
          ment and testing.
I will care for you in sickness, enjoy you
          in health,
give thanks for you always, and with a glad heart
I shall treasure you all the days of our lives.

This is my heartfelt promise. This is my solemn
vow.

## The Blessing of the Rings

Wholeness is the state in which nothing is missing and everything is possible, in which what has been is completed by what is, and in which there is no lack. These rings represent wholeness, a coming around of the cycle: from sickness to health, from want to plenty, from despair to joy, from failure to possibility, from loneliness to love.

Let these rings also be a sign that love has substance as well as soul, a present as well as a past, and that, despite its sometimes sorrows love is a circle of happiness, wonder, and delight.

## The Exchanging of the Rings

I give you this ring as a token of my abiding love, as a sign that I have chosen you above all others, that we shall together go through more than we have already been through, and of the hope that the treasures of our future shall render invisible the sorrows of our past.

I love you.

## The Pronouncement of Marriage

Now, because you have chosen one another, honored each other with the precious gift of your rings, and pledged to love each other for all the days of your life, it gives me great joy to pronounce you husband and wife (married). You may kiss.

## The Kiss

## The Benediction

May the higher power that has given you the gift of healing and the miracle of this marriage, guard your well-being and fill your days with joy and happiness in the presence of one another. Go in peace; live in joy. Thanks be to God.

# Ceremonial Flourishes

*T*he following are a number of suggestions for other ritual elements you may want to add to your ceremony. As you will see, their general function is to involve the guests more fully in your celebration.

Since a wedding is a gathering of loved ones on behalf of the two individuals being married, the presence of your guests is neither neutral nor irrelevant. You seek their blessing; you desire their witness. In exchange for honoring you with the benediction of their presence, you inspire them with the example of your love, and the more they can join in the ceremony itself, the more the experience will be heartfelt both for you and for them.

1. Before you say your vows, tell a vignette or a little bit of your love story in front of the congregation. There's nothing so delightful

as a love story, and telling yours not only will remind you of why you're getting married, but remembering the sweet early days of your romance will also give you a wonderful feeling. It will also delight and inspire the people celebrating with you to be let in on the secrets of your love story.

2. Before or after you recite your own vows, invite the married people at your wedding to stand with their partners and reaffirm their own vows. You can have the officiant prepare some special words for them. For example, "I love you and acknowledge you and thank you again for the gift of your love. Thank you for being there all along the way, in public and in private, tenderly and fiercely, always steadfast in your love. What an incredible gift!"

This is a lovely way of allowing your guests to use your wedding as an occasion for renewing their own relationships, inspired by your example in articulating your vows for the first time.

3. Write a special song or poem for your wedding, or rewrite the lyrics to an old favorite

song: ("The New Year's Eve we did the town . . ., the night we tore the goal post down . . .") Such a specially created piece can tell the story of your relationship in particular or it can extol the virtues of love and marriage in general. Words tailored to your unique experience will give a touching personal note to your wedding.

Fred, a musician, wrote and performed a beautiful song when he married Susie in an outdoor wedding. It chronicled all the special events and magical feelings of their courtship and it was a smash hit not only for Susie but for all their guests.

4. Each of you may want to choose a moment in which to make a personal tribute to your parents. For example, if the bride has her father give her away, she may want to turn to him and say, "By the way, Dad, thanks for being such a great father all these years. You were a wonderful example of a loving man, and a hard act to follow, I might add. And Mom, thanks for always taking such good care of me. I wouldn't be here without all the wonderful love you showered on me."

The point here is to make some very specific expression of appreciation which tells your parents how much you treasure and value them for all they did to bring you to this place. Include some very special memories that will touch their hearts and truly acknowledge how much you value them.

5. You may also want to thank your spouse's parents for all they did to turn him or her into the wonderful person you're marrying. "Thanks for bringing Joel into the world, for giving him all the love you did to turn him into the man who's irresistible to me. Thank you for loving him first. I promise to try to keep up your good work," or, "Thanks for being such great parents. Without your love, I know she wouldn't be the wonderful person I'm marrying today."

While all these sweet things could of course be said at the reception—or at the rehearsal dinner for that matter—saying them at the wedding, in front of all the people who are sharing this experience with you, suddenly takes them to a very touching depth. You enlarge your circle of intimacy and create a deeper bond with your new parents-in-law and your parents by speaking so feelingly to them in the presence of so many listeners. Besides, these are the kinds of words parents wait a lifetime to hear. They did deliver you to this occasion—and they do deserve some thanks.

6. Invite your parents to tell a story or share a reminiscence about you. This is a beautiful way for them to go through a conscious tiny ceremony of letting go of you, and also of reaffirming their special relationship with you. They can do this at the moment of giving away the bride and/or groom, or just before the address. This is a lovely way of inviting your new spouse into some of the secrets of your childhood. For example, "David always talked about growing up and marrying a beautiful princess. I'm so happy to see that his childhood dream is coming true."

Or it can take the form of a little inside advice. John's mother, for example, turned to his new wife Sara and said, "He's always late, but don't take it personally. It doesn't mean he doesn't love you." And Sara's mother told John, "She's a wonderful cook and she'll be happy to spoil you, but she'll spoil you longer—and better—if you take her out to dinner one night a week."

Once again, these words will be all the more touching if spoken in the presence of witnesses. The guests at your ceremony serve to deliver energy, to invest what is spoken with a meaning that is driven home.

7. Your parents can welcome the new member into the family. Your father may want to say for example, "Neil, it is with great joy that I welcome you into our family. I look forward to knowing you and to loving you as my new son" or, "Jan, we're so happy to have you join us as a daughter. Our hearts are open to you and we look forward to sharing our lives with you over the coming years."

8. Another lovely idea is to keep an on-the-spot record of your wedding. Buy a beautiful blank book and appoint one of your attendants or a special guest to be the "recorder" at the ceremony and reception, to write down all the memorable things said by the guests as they experience your wedding. Pick someone who has

a nice sense of what is important and allow him or her to choose what to record of what is said about you, about the wedding itself, the ceremony, the gown, the gorgeous flowers, the wonderful sermon, or the great appetizers. While you may have photographs and/or a videotape of your wedding, it's lovely to lie in bed afterward, turning the pages of a little book where all the sweet, amusing, and interesting remarks about your wedding have been hand-recorded.

9. Circulate a special book among your guests and invite them, in the mode of a high school autograph party, to record their comments and good wishes for you. Of course many guests will have already included their wishes on cards or with their gifts, but having a book specifically for this purpose will bring together in a single place words from the entire community that shared this precious occasion with you. I especially like this idea because it allows you to remember the whole texture of the experience, including the people whose presence helped to create it.

10. Read a poem, the lyrics of a song, or a

brief paragraph that has moved you, and tell your partner how this expresses your feelings about him or her on the occasion of your wedding. In other words, make a mini-sermon of your own. Don't be afraid to make your ceremony really personal, to use it as an opportunity to express the deep and special feelings you hold in your heart for the person you are marrying.

All too often we are embarrassed about our feelings, as if the things that move us most deeply, that touch our hearts and change our lives, should somehow be shrouded in secrecy. But this is your wedding after all, the most touching occasion of your life. Saying these things now will create the unforgettable catchwords and phrases that you can treasure as little love talismans throughout the days of your married life.

11. Since weddings often represent great expense and personal indulgence, couples may want to use their wedding as an opportunity to take note of the hardship of others and as an occasion to share their resources. Therefore, you may want to pause at a certain point in your ceremony to express thanks for your good for-

tune and encourage the congregation to make a contribution in your name for the homeless, or to a charity of your choice.

You may want to mention this in your wedding invitation. For example, "May we ask that you make a donation to those who don't share our many blessings. We will provide a basket for this purpose at the reception. This is our way of sharing our good fortune with the world, and of starting out our marriage with the recognition that none of us is separate from the whole."

12. Pass the peace. Before or after the Convocation you might want to have the officiant suggest that each person turn to the person closest to him or her and embrace and say a few words of greeting or blessing. This will more closely unite those who are celebrating your marriage with you.

13. If you are a woman, a short while before the wedding, you might like to join with some women friends for a special ceremony of blessing. Men have bachelor parties, but aside from showers, where the focus is on building a

dowry, women rarely have an opportunity to send off the sister who is getting married.

For example, Lydia chose to meet with her friends on the beach and asked each of them to bring a natural object (a shell, a leaf, a stone) that had meaning for her. Sitting in a circle after sharing a meal, each one of her friends spoke a blessing to Lydia that was symbolized by the object. Afterward they gathered the items into a velvet bag for her to keep.

As you depart the community of single women and join ranks with your spouse in married life, you may want to do something similar by preparing a special ritual to serve as your rite of passage. Think of exactly how you would like this mini-ceremony to be conducted, and send invitations to your special women friends to share it with you.

14. If you are marrying again and have children, whether grown or small, you may want to invite them to say a few words—of welcome, of well-wishing, or of celebration—at your wedding ceremony: "Well, Mom, you've finally found the man of your dreams" or, "Dad,

I'm really glad you found Julie. You two are wonderful together." You may also want them to serve as your attendants or to fulfill the function of "giving you away."

Whatever the form it takes, do invite your children to participate in the ceremony, not only so they won't feel left out but also because our children so often deliver the startling insights that with a lifetime of thinking we could never arrive at ourselves.

15. Do something festive or offbeat. Suzanne and Philip had an outdoor garden wedding and at the altar constructed a maypole with colored ribbons. Before exchanging their rings, with a beautiful recording of renaissance music playing in the background, they wove the streamers of the maypole together, symbolizing their union, the weaving together of their lives.

16. Consider making a whole weekend of your wedding with a small group of family and friends. Rent a block of hotel rooms (Motel 6 or The Palace, depending on your budget) or a series of campsites and allow people to share several days of the wedding experience with you.

To do so creates, in a way that is nearly impossible otherwise, an experience of almost tribal bonding. As the tribe is gradually drawn together, the web of its support is strengthened until, by the time the wedding actually occurs, you will have surrounded yourself with a most beautiful and powerful matrix of blessings, and those who have shared the time with you will have forged greater bonds of friendship and love.

17. Prepare a special garment or talisman for your sweetheart to wear or carry at the wedding. Amanda, who was married in a flower-filled meadow, hand embroidered a shirt for her husband to wear. On the inside band of the collar she embroidered a heart, the words, " I love you," and the date of their wedding. Lance prepared a exquisite "scepter of flowers" for Gwen. Rather than having her bouquet arranged by a florist, he fashioned a tower of roses laced with ribbon streamers, delivering his love and his creativity to her in this most special of ways.

18. You may want to have your pet participate in some gracious way in your wedding

ceremony. Suzette, who has three elegant whip-
pets, had them precede her down the aisle at her
outdoor garden wedding. Lucinda and Reg had a
cage of white love birds ensconced in a flower-
bedecked arch at the front of the church for their
afternoon wedding.

19. If appropriate, be daring and ask a
man to be your bridesmaid. Elizabeth's older
brother had always been her dearest most nurturing friend, and so she asked him, and not one
of her girlfriends, to be the attendant of honor at
her wedding.

20. After reciting your vows, have the
officiant address your guests and challenge them
to make a vow of support to you. After all, it is
within the context of this community that your
marriage will be enacted. For example, "Now that
you have heard _____ and _____ recite their vows,
do you, their family and friends, promise from
this day forward, so long as you shall know
them, to encourage them and love them, to give
them your guidance and support in being true
and steadfast in the promises that they have
made here in your presence?" "We do."

21. Personally greet your guests at some early point in the ceremony. After they walked down the aisle together, Jill and Scott turned to the congregation and went aisle by aisle welcoming each person individually and thanking them for coming to the wedding before proceeding with the ceremony. This is a beautiful way to bring the congregation together, a chance for every person who shares the occasion to feel bonded to the purposes of the witnessing community.

22. Add a fanciful, even theatrical touch to your wedding. A wedding is first of all a ceremony and therefore you have free rein to include any elements you'd like to elevate the ritual. Jessica and Paul, who were married in Renaissance costumes on her parent's sweeping lawn, had a lutenist and a band of jugglers strolling among and entertaining the guests before they walked down the petal-strewn aisle. Later they introduced a baroque string quartet and trumpets, changing the mood in preparation for the more serious aspects of the ceremony.

What they communicated with their

playful jugglers was more than that marriage is a
juggling act; they reminded themselves and their
guests that marriage is an enterprise both serious
and playful, fanciful and holy. And rather than
speaking to this truth, they had it very imagina-
tively dramatized.

23. You may wish to have an attendant or
two read, in a performance mode, one or more
selections from works on love and marriage.
Remember again that a wedding is one of those
very rare occasions we have to enact our ceremonial impulses, and you don't have to rush
through it.

Hearing more than one meditation on the
meaning of love will be an experience of great
value, not only for you, but also for the people
sharing this experience with you. We all need to
be reminded that love is powerful and real, and
that marriage is a holy and beautiful undertaking.
Hearing poetic words on the subject is one of the
most deeply moving reminders we can have.

24. As the wedding begins, instead of
walking down the aisle, consider positioning
yourselves at opposite ends of the altar, signify-

ing that in marriage we join one another from the distance of our individuality. As you gradually approach one another, have the officiant speak a few words about how in true marriage we never become completely dissolved in one another, but retain our individual selves even as we are united with our beloved.

25. At a designated point in the ceremony, perhaps at the beginning or end, invite the congregation to join you in singing a song, the words of which you have printed in advance and distributed to the guests. There is nothing like music in general, and singing in particular, to create an emotional bond—to draw us together in a single breath of love.

# Additional Vows
## and Other Promises

I give you my love
I give you my heart
I give you my hope
I give you with joy
   from the coffers of my precious time
   the rest of the days of my life;
To delight in your body
To nourish your mind
To be at home with your spirit
   the way a star is at home in the sky;
To celebrate you with joy
   the way the sun emblazons the sea
   with its light;
To console you in sorrow
To wrap my heart around yours
   like a blanket
Until we both shall grow old
   and the sight fall

      from our eyes and our being
        fall from life to light;
I choose to go with you always
from this day until the end of our days
as your adoring husband (wife/mate).


\*\*\*

In the name of God,
I \_\_\_\_ take you \_\_\_\_,
to be my beloved wife (husband/mate).


To stand with you in the bond of the love that
binds us,
to honor you, to change with you,
to open the windows of my heart,
to behold the highest meanings of our being,
to learn compassion with you,
to be one with you in the all, to suffer with you,
to be kind.


I promise you this with my soul
from my heart
till death do us part.

\*\*\*

Because I have never known such a love
I take you now to be forever
my wife (husband/companion).

I long to know you,
I desire to discover you.
I promise to honor you, to mirror
you in the beautiful uniqueness of your spirit,
to thank you when you delight me,
to forgive you when you offend me,
to receive you as the fulfillment
of all my lessons,
the chalice of all my joy.

Therefore, do I give myself to you now
in this consecrated state of being married,
to hold you in my heart, to protect you
with the wings of my soul, to be blessed
by the gift of your love
for all the days of my life.

***

Before God and these our witnesses,
this is my solemn promise:
to love you and hold you always
          as my wife (husband);
to stand beside you in good times
and bad
because my love is so great, and
your presence such a miracle;
to be sweet with you and fierce
          with you,
to nourish you with my gentleness,
to uphold you with my strength,
to go with you through all the
          changings of age and of infirmity,
whatever the sorrows or losses,
until we become pure spirits
in the end.

***

My love
I waited so long for you
that I had begun to believe
there was no such thing as true love,

that my life would be lived out
alone, that nothing precious
would come in the form
of someone to love.

Finally, after many sorrows
        and missteps and losses,
after I had given up all hope,
you were given to me like
a miracle, like a single
elegant star in the darkest
of nights

Now I feel joy
Now I feel whole
Now I feel that anything
is possible

Thank you for coming
into my life; thank you
for loving me well.
I have waited so long for my heart
to be glad,  for my soul
to be full.

Thank you for coming
into my life.  Thank you
for coming into
my love.

*** 

I _____ take you _____,
from this day forward and into
the long forever to be my beloved,
my sweetheart, my darling, my wife (husband/
        mate).

I promise always to love you
to honor you, to adore you
to give thanks for the gift
of your presence.

We have come so far
against so many odds
and I choose to go
with you always
from now until the end
of my life.

\*\*\*

Startled awake
at this late and unexpectedly beautiful
hour, long after sorrow, long after
love, long after hope,
I receive you into the breath
of my soul
to make my light with you,
to fill with joy my glad heart,
and to love you far more and dearly
than ever before in all your
imaginings you could have imagined;

with the sight of my eyes, with
the wings of my heart, with
the milk of my soul.

I have come to you
with the plain grace
of a small bird
to love you
and I will
love you:

honor you and adore you
and with my body console
you, and with my mind embrace
the unrepeatable refinements
of your being.

So will I love you,
so will I be your father  mother  sister  brother
        lover  son  (daughter)
soul of your soul will I kin of your kin be
in sleeksilver weather and greybleeding times.
I will keepsake your heart in my soul, in
the palms of my eyes in the small
of my hand;

I will love you
as the hawk flies high and floating circle
in the blue sky bowled intelligent
and endlessly alive above us,
till the wingspan stilled falls
and the new night starry bright
incomprehensible and distant

beautifully bows down
and frees us from the earth
sun moon sky
and takes us   wakes us
and as stars we are reborn.


***


I ____ take you ____ ,
To be my beloved wife (husband/mate)
To give you the gift of my
        most tender love
To honor you with my body
To fill up the wounds
        in your heart;

In good times and bad
When things go easy with us
and when they are difficult;

When love is a gift
and when it is an effort;
When we are successful and
        prosperous

and when the wolf of uncertainty
        lurks at the door.

I promise always
        to love you
        to cherish you
        to hold you always in highest regard, and
        to die with this love that I have for you
        untarnished in my heart.

***

Now do I marry you,
now do I take you forever
into my heart, and loving you now
I promise that I shall be steadfast
always in my love.

You are my princess, my darling, my queen
        (my prince, my knight, my king)

my companion, my consort, my most highly
honored person,
So do I choose you, so do I love you,
so do I promise, from this day forward

to be your most cherishing husband (wife/mate).

\*\*\*

\_\_\_\_, my beloved,
I choose now to take this journey
    with you
wherever it leads
whatever the outcome
no matter what may befall us
as God is my witness
through all the days
of our lives.

\*\*\*

I \_\_\_\_ take thee \_\_\_\_,
to be my partner in marriage
and in life

To love you and honor you
To give thanks for you and
To serve you
    with my wit
    my strength
    my heart

To stand by you always
> even if sickness should threaten
> and despite the turmoil around us

To create with you a living example
of the beauty of a relationship
between a man and a woman

***

I promise to listen to you
To labor with you
To encourage you

To believe in you even
> when you doubt yourself

To be the mirror
> of your highest value

And to hold myself beside you
until the gates of death.

## *Exchanging of the Rings Suggestions*

As the sign from my heart
that I desire to live with you
from this day forward as my wife (husband/
    mate),
and that you may remember forever
that I have chosen you above all others,
I give you this ring as a sign of my love.

***

This ring is my precious gift to you,
as a measure of my love and as a sign
that from this day forward your every breath
shall be surrounded by my love.

***

I give you this ring as a sign
that I choose you for love
to be your partner and husband (wife/mate)
today, tomorrow, and always.

\*\*\*

I marry you with this ring,
with my heart,
with my body,
and with all the syllables
of my soul.

\*\*\*

As a symbol
of how endlessly happy you make me
and of how crazy I am about you,
I give you this ring, my dear sweetheart,
so you and the whole world will know
how much and for always I love you.

\*\*\*

I give you this ring
as the symbol that
I have cast my lot with
yours, that I am bound
to you always, through my love,
with my soul, and all my heart.

# Postlude

May your wedding
bring you happiness

May your marriage
bring you boundless joy.

# Your Personal Notes